D1571418

SUREFIRE STUDY SUCCESS

SUREFIRE TIPS TO IMPROVE YOUR
READING
SKILLS

RON FRY

ROSEN
PUBLISHING®

New York

This edition published in 2016 by:

The Rosen Publishing Group, Inc.

29 East 21st Street

New York, NY 10010

Additional end matter copyright © 2016 by The Rosen Publishing Group, Inc.

Library of Congress Cataloging-in-Publication Date

Fry, Ronald W.
 Surefire tips to improve your reading skills / Ron Fry.
     pages cm -- ((Surefire study success))
 Includes bibliographical references and index.
 ISBN 978-1-5081-7094-5 (library binding)
 1. Reading comprehension -- Juvenile literature. I. Fry, Ron. II. Title.
 LB1050.45 F79 2016
 428.4'3--d23

Manufactured in the United States of America

First published as *Improve Your Reading* by Cengage Learning,
copyright © 2012 Ron Fry.

CONTENTS

FOREWORD

READ ON!

A number of you are students, not just the high school students I always thought were my readers, but also college students making up for study skills you may have lacked in high school, and middle school students trying to master these study skills early in your educational career to maximize your opportunities for success.

If you're a high school student, you should be particularly comfortable with both the language and format of this book—its relatively short sentences and paragraphs, occasionally humorous (hopefully) headings and subheadings, and a reasonable but certainly not outrageous vocabulary. I wrote it with you in mind!

If you're a middle school student, I doubt you'll have trouble with the concepts or language in this book. Sixth, seventh, and eighth grade is the perfect time to learn the different ways to read and the methods to better retain whatever you're reading.

Do not pass "Go." Take the time to learn these skills now. You may have been able to kid yourself that mediocre or even poor reading skills didn't stop you from finishing, perhaps even succeeding in, high school. I guarantee you will not be able to kid anyone in college. You must master all of the skills in this book to survive, let alone succeed.

Some Random Thoughts About Learning

Learning shouldn't be painful and certainly doesn't have to be boring, though it's far too often both. It's not necessarily going to be wonderful and painless, either. Sometimes you actually have to work hard to figure something out or get a project done. That is reality.

It's also reality that everything isn't readily apparent or easily understandable. That's okay. You will learn how to get past the confusion. Heck, if you actually think you're supposed to understand everything you read the first time through, you're kidding yourself. Learning something slowly doesn't mean there's something wrong with you. It may be a subject that virtually everybody learns slowly. A good student just takes his time, follows a reasonable plan, and remains confident that the lightbulb of understanding will eventually click on.

Parents often ask me, "How can I motivate my teenager?" My initial response is usually to smile and say, "If I knew the answer to that question, I would have retired very wealthy quite some time ago." I think there is an answer, but it's not something parents can do—it's something the student has to decide: Are you going to spend the school day interested and alert or bored and resentful?

It's really that simple. Since you have to go to school anyway, why not develop the attitude that you might as well be active and learn as much as possible instead of being miserable? The difference between a C and an A or B for many students is, I firmly believe, merely a matter of wanting to do better. As I constantly stress in radio and TV interviews, inevitably you will leave school. And very quickly, you'll discover all anyone really cares about is what you know and what you can do. Grades won't count anymore; neither will tests. So you can learn it all now or regret it later.

How many times have you said to yourself, "I don't know why I'm bothering trying to learn this calculus (algebra, geometry, physics, chemistry, history, whatever). I'll never use this again!"? The truth is, you have no clue what you're going to need to know tomorrow or next week, let alone next year or in a decade.

I've been amazed in my own life how things I did with no specific purpose in mind (except probably to earn money or meet a girl) turned out years later to be not just invaluable to my life or career, but essential. How was I to know when I took German as my language elective in high school that the most important international trade show in book publishing was in Frankfurt, Germany? Or that the basic skills I learned one year working for an accountant (while I was writing my first book) would become essential when I later started four companies? Or how important basic math skills would be in selling and negotiating over the years? (Okay, I'll admit it: I haven't used a differential equation in 20 years, but, hey, you never know!)

So learn it all. And don't be surprised if the subject you'd vote "least likely to ever be useful" winds up being the key to your fame and fortune.

There Aren't Many Study Rules

Though I immodestly maintain that my *How to Study* Program is the most helpful to the most people, there are certainly plenty of other purported study books out there.

Inevitably, these other books promote the authors' "system," which usually means what they did to get through school. This "system," whether basic and traditional or wildly quirky, may or may not work for you. So what do you do if "their" way of taking notes makes no sense to you? Or you master their highfalutin' "Super Student Study Symbols" and still get Cs?

There are very few "rights" and "wrongs" out there in the study world. There's certainly no single "right" way to attack a multiple choice test or take notes. So don't get fooled into thinking there is, especially if what you're doing seems to be working for you.

Needless to say, don't read my books looking for that single, inestimable system of "rules" that will work for everyone. You won't find it, 'cause there's no such bird. You will find a plethora of techniques, tips, tricks, gimmicks, and what-have-you, some or all of which may work for you, some of which won't. Pick and choose, change and adapt, figure out what works for you. Because you are the one responsible for creating your study system, not me.

I've used the phrase "Study smarter, not harder" as a sort of catch phrase in promotion and publicity for my program for two decades. So what does it mean to you? Does it mean I guarantee you'll spend less time studying? Or that the least amount of time is best? Or that studying isn't ever supposed to be difficult?

Hardly. It does mean that studying inefficiently is wasting time that could be spent doing other (okay, probably more fun) things and that getting your studying done as quickly and efficiently as possible is a realistic, worthy, and attainable goal. I'm no stranger to hard work, but I'm not a monastic dropout who thrives on self-flagellation. I try not to work harder than I have to!

It's a Hard-Wired World

In 1988, when I wrote my first book I composed it, formatted it, and printed it on (gasp) a personal computer. Most people did not have a computer, let alone a neighborhood network and DSL, or surf the Internet, or chat online, or Instant Message their friends, or read hundreds of books on a Kindle, or…you get the point.

Those days are very dead and gone. And you should cheer, even if you aren't sure what DOS was (is? could be?). Because the spread of the personal computer and, even more important, the Internet, has taken studying from the Dark Ages to the Info Age in merely a decade.

As a result, you will find all of my books assume you have a computer and know how to use it—for note taking, reading, writing papers, researching, and much more. There are many tasks that may be harder on a computer—and I'll point them out—but don't believe for a second that a computer won't help you tremendously, whatever your age, whatever your grades.

As for the Internet, it has absolutely revolutionized research. Whether you're writing a paper, putting together a reading list, studying for the SAT, or just trying to organize your life, it has become a more valuable tool than the greatest library in the world. Heck, it *is* the greatest library in the world…and more. So if you are not Internet-savvy, admit it, get a book (over the Internet, of course), and get wired. You'll be missing far too much—and be studying far harder—without it.

The Last Commerical

I can guarantee that my books contain the most wide-ranging, comprehensive, and complete system of studying ever published. I have attempted to create a system that is usable, useful, practical, and learnable. One that you can use—whatever your age, whatever your level of achievement, whatever your IQ—to start doing better in school, in work, and in life immediately.

Good luck.

Ron Fry

CHAPTER 1

THE BASIS OF ALL
STUDY SKILLS

I think you'll find this is a book unlike any you've read before. And if you take the time to read it, I promise it will make everything else you have to read—whatever your student status, whatever your job, whatever your age— a lot easier to get through.

Why? Because I'm going to show you how to plow through all your reading assignments—whatever the subjects— better and faster... and how to remember more of what you read.

This book is not a gimmicky speed-reading method. It's not a spelling and grammar guide. Nor is it a lecture on the joys of reading. It's a practical guide, geared to you— a student of who isn't necessarily a poor reader, but who wants to get more from reading and do better in school and in life.

Personally, I'll read just about anything handy, just to be able to read something. But just because I have always loved to read, it didn't make it any easier to face some of those deadly textbook reading assignments. As a student, you will inevitably be required, as I was, to spend hours poring through ponderous, fact-filled, convoluted reading assignments for subjects that are required, but not exactly scintillating.

You may love reading for pleasure but have trouble reading textbook assignments for certain subjects. You may get the reading done but forget what you've read nearly as quickly as you read it. Or you just may hate the thought of sitting still to read anything. Whatever kind of student you are—and whatever your level of reading skill—I've written this book to help you surmount your reading challenge, whatever it may be.

You'll learn what you should read—and what you don't have to. You'll discover how to cut down on the time you spend reading, how to identify the main idea in your reading, as well as the important details, and how to remember more of what you read.

I'll show you different ways to read various types of books, from dry science texts to cumbersome classics.

Who knows? I might even convince you that reading is fun!

When you're a good reader, the world is your oyster—you qualify for better schools, better jobs, better pay. Poor readers qualify for poor jobs and less fulfilling lives.

Ready to Begin? Get Motivated!

Any attempt to improve your reading must begin with motivation. Reading is not a genetic trait that is written in your DNA—there's no gene that makes you a good or bad reader like the ones that decide your hair or eye color. For the most part, reading is an acquired skill—a skill you can secure, grow, and sharpen. You just have to want to.

Good Reader vs. Poor Reader

Look at the following comparison of a good reader and a poor reader as if you were some corporate hotshot who could hire just one of the individuals.

Good Reader: You read for purpose. You've clearly defined your reason for reading—a question you want answered, facts you must remember, ideas you need to grasp, current events that affect you, or just the pleasure of following a well-written story.

Poor Reader: Yes, you read, but often have no real reason for doing so. You aimlessly struggle through assigned reading, with little effort to grasp the "message."

Good Reader: You read and digest the concepts and ideas the author is trying to communicate.

Poor Reader: You get lost in the muddle of words, struggling to make sense of what the author is trying to say. You are often bored because you force yourself to read every word to "get the message"…which you usually don't.

Good Reader: You read critically and ask questions to evaluate whether the author's arguments are reasonable or totally off-the-wall. You recognize biases and don't just "believe" everything you read.

Poor Reader: You suffer from the delusion that everything in print is true and are easily swayed from what you formerly believed to be true by any argument that sounds good.

Good Reader: You read a variety of books, magazines, and newspapers and enjoy all types of reading—fiction, poetry, biography, current events.

Poor Reader: You're a one-track reader—you read the sports pages, comics, or Gothic novels. Current events? You catch updates about your world from TV news "sound bites."

Good Reader: You enjoy reading and embrace it as an essential tool in your desire to better yourself.

Poor Reader: You hate to read, deeming it a chore to be endured only when you have to. Reading is "boring."

Take a minute and ask yourself, whom would you hire? Yes, you might hire Mr. Poor Reader...in some low-paying job. But would you ever put someone with such low-level skills in a position of major responsibility?

At this point, I won't ask you to evaluate your own level of reading skills. Characterizing yourself as a "good" or "poor" reader was not the point of this exercise. What is important is to realize that Ms. Good Reader didn't spring full-blown from Zeus's cranium quoting Shakespearean sonnets and reading physics texts for fun. She learned to read the same way you and I did—with "See Spot run."

In time and through making reading a habit, Ms. Good Reader acquired and honed a skill that will open a world of opportunity to her.

Mr. Poor Reader, at some point, decided that being a good reader was not worth the effort and made poor reading his habit.

The good news is that being a poor reader is not a life sentence—you can improve your reading. The challenge is to find the motivation!

How Fast Can You Understand?

When we read too fast or too slowly,
we understand nothing.
—Pascal

Are you worried that you read too slowly? You probably shouldn't be—less rapid readers are not necessarily less able. What counts is what you comprehend and remember. And like anything else, practice will probably increase your speed levels. If you must have a ranking, read the 500-word selection that follows (adapted from *American Firsts* by Stephen Spignesi, published by New Page Books, 2004) from start to finish, noting the elapsed time on your watch. Score yourself as follows:

45 seconds or less	very fast
46–60 seconds	fast
61–90 seconds	high average
91–119 seconds	average
120–150 seconds	slow
151 seconds or more	very slow

The original incarnation of Coca-Cola contained cocaine, a common ingredient of patent medicines in the late 19th century. The drug was so beloved and believed to be so beneficial that the early ads for Coca-Cola pitched it as a "brain tonic." Cocaine did what cocaine does: It made people more alert and focused; it elevated mood (to the point of euphoria); it eliminated fatigue and had something of an analgesic effect. Who knew it was addictive?

Eventually everyone did, and over the past century, the Coca-Cola company has worked very hard to eliminate any traces of cocaine from the beverage. However, cocaine is found in the cola nut (a seed of the coca leaf) and it is therefore impossible to remove it entirely. The amount of cocaine in Coca-Cola is so miniscule, however, as to be immeasurable; by any and all standards, Coca-Cola is cocaine free. It is not caffeine free, though, because this stimulant is also found in the coca leaf and no attempt is made to remove it for regular Coke. It is removed, though, for production of caffeine-free cola beverages.

Coca-Cola is the world's most recognized trademark. Some estimates claim that 94 percent of the world's population recognizes the Coca-Cola name and/or distinctive Spencerian Script logo. The original formula for Coca-Cola syrup was concocted by Dr. John Pemberton in his Atlanta, Georgia backyard in early May 1885. (Today, the secret formula of Coke is known as "7X.") He used a three-legged kettle, and his bookkeeper Frank Robinson not only came up with the name, but also drew the first script version of the product's name. The syrup was mixed with water and first sold to the thirsty at the soda fountain in Jacob's Pharmacy in Atlanta on May 8, 1885. It was touted as a brain and nerve tonic, but Pemberton lost money in his first year selling the drink.

Legend has it that Pemberton saw one of his employees adding carbonated seltzer water to the "tonic," and the Coke we know today was born. Today, Coca-Cola is the most popular beverage in the world. More than one billion Cokes are consumed every day, and it has become known as the quintessential American drink. Coca-Cola's strongest competitor is Pepsi®. There are differences between the two colas, though, and many people have a favorite. Coke has a heavier, more carbonated taste and feel, and an orange-based flavor tone beneath the vanilla and cola flavors. Pepsi is lighter and sweeter, and uses a lemon-lime flavor tone beneath its cola flavoring. Also, Coke has 47 milligrams of caffeine per 12 ounce serving, compared to Pepsi's 37 milligrams. Both have about 39 grams of sugar.

These days, there is also an enormous, worldwide Coca-Cola subculture. The Coke logo has been licensed for use on a slew of products, and there are collectors all over the world who seek out these items and often pay top dollar for them. A recent search for Coke products on eBay® returned more than 30,000 individual items.

Now answer the questions on the following page without referring back to the text:

1. What stimulant besides cocaine is found in the coca leaf?
   A. Ecstasy
   B. Caffeine
   C. Ephedrine
   D. Cola

2. About how long has Coke been around?
   A. 85 years
   B. 185 years
   C. 120 years
   D. 88 years

3. What flavors are mentioned as existing in Coke (vs. Pepsi)?
   A. Vanilla, cola, and lemon-lime
   B. Cola and vanilla
   C. Vanilla, cola, and orange
   D. Orange and cola

4. Which has more sugar: Coke or Pepsi?
   A. Coke
   B. Pepsi
   C. Both
   D. Neither

A good reader should be reading fast or very fast and have gotten at least three of the four questions correct.

Answers to Quiz: 1) B; 2) C; 3) C; 4) C

You should only worry—and plan to do something about it—if you fall in the slow or very slow range and/or missed two or more questions. Otherwise, you are probably reading as fast as you need to and retaining most of what you read.

Again, the relationship between speed and comprehension is paramount: Read too fast and you may comprehend less; reading more slowly does not necessarily mean you're not grasping the material.

What *Decreases* Reading Speed/Comprehension:

1. Reading aloud or moving your lips when you read.
2. Reading mechanically—using your finger to follow words, moving your head as you read.
3. Applying the wrong kind of reading to the material.
4. Lacking sufficient vocabulary.

There are several things you can do to improve these reading mechanics.

To Increase Your Reading Speed:

1. Focus your attention and concentration.
2. Eliminate outside distractions.
3. Provide for an uncluttered, comfortable environment.
4. Don't get hung up on single words or sentences, but do look up (in the dictionary) key words that you must understand in order to grasp an entire concept.
5. Try to grasp overall concepts rather than attempting to understand every detail.

6. If you find yourself moving your lips when you read (vocalization), practice reading with a pen or some other (nontoxic, nonsugary) object in your mouth. If it falls out while you're reading, you know you have to keep working!

7. Work on building your vocabulary. You may be reading slowly (and/or having trouble understanding what you read) because your vocabulary is insufficient for your reading level.

8. Read more…and more often. Reading is a habit that improves with practice.

9. Avoid rereading words or phrases. According to one recent study, an average student reading at 250 words per minute rereads 20 times per page. The slowest readers reread the most.

To Increase Comprehension:

1. Try to make the act of learning sequential—comprehension is built by adding new knowledge to existing knowledge.

2. Review and rethink at designated points in your reading. Test yourself to see if the importance of the material is getting through.

3. If things don't add up, discard your conclusions. Go back, reread, and try to find an alternate conclusion.

4. Summarize what you've read, rephrasing it in your notes in your own words.

Most importantly, read at the speed that's comfortable for you. Though I can read extremely fast, I choose to read novels much more slowly so I can appreciate the author's wordplay. Likewise, any material that I find particularly difficult to grasp slows me right down. I read newspapers, popular magazines, and the like very fast, seeking to grasp the information but not worrying about every detail.

Should you take some sort of speed reading course, especially if your current speed level is low?

Reading for speed has some merit—many people who are slow readers read as little as possible, simply because they find it so tedious and boring. But just reading faster is not the answer to becoming a good reader.

I can't see that such a course could particularly hurt you in any way. I can also, however, recommend that you simply keep practicing reading, which will increase your speed naturally.

Don't Remember Less...Faster

Retention is primarily a product of what you understand. It has little to do with how fast you read, how great an outline you can construct, or how many fluorescent colors you use to mark your textbooks. Reading a text, grasping the message, and remembering it are the fundamentals that make for high-level retention. Reading at a 1,000-words-per-minute clip does not necessarily mean that you have a clue as to what a text really says.

If you can read an assignment faster than anyone in class, but can't give a one sentence synopsis of what you just read, your high reading rate is inconsequential. If you (eventually) get the author's message—even if it takes you an hour or two longer than some of your friends—your time will pay off in huge dividends in class and later in life.

That's why this book concentrates only on how you as a student can increase what you retain from your reading assignments. Whether you're reading a convoluted textbook that bores even the professor to tears or a magazine article, newspaper feature, or novel, you follow a certain process to absorb what you've read, which consists of:

1. Grasping the main idea.
2. Gathering the facts.
3. Figuring out the sequence of events.
4. Drawing conclusions.

When you spend an hour reading an assignment and then can't recall what you've just read, it's usually because a link in this chain has been broken. You've skipped one of these crucial steps in your reading process, leaving your understanding of the material filled with gaps.

To increase your retention rate, you need to master each level in this chain of comprehension. Not everything you read will require that you comprehend on all four levels. Following a set of cooking directions, for example, simply requires that you discern the sequence for combining all the ingredients. Other reading will demand that you be able to compile facts, identify a thesis, and give some critical thought as to its validity.

Ms. Good Reader is not only able to perform at each level of comprehension, but also has developed an instinct: She recognizes that certain things she reads can be read just to gather facts or just to grasp the main idea. She then is able to read quickly to accomplish this goal and move on to her next assignment—or to that Steven King novel she's been dying to read.

The first chapters of this book will address these different steps and provide exercises designed to help you master each stage in the process of retaining what you read.

In the final chapters, we will look at how to read literature, how to read a math or science textbook, and how to outline so that you can easily review a text.

By the time you finish this short book, you should find that, by following the procedures I've suggested, you have significantly improved your reading comprehension.

Finding Other Textbooks

Few textbooks are written by what most of us would even remotely call professional writers. While the authors and editors might well be experts, even legends, in a particular subject, writing in jargon-free, easy-to-grasp prose is probably not their strong suit. You will occasionally be assigned a textbook that is so obtuse you aren't even sure whether to read it front to back, upside down, or inside out.

If you find a particular chapter, section, or entire textbook as tough to read as getting your baby brother to do you a favor, get to the library or a bookstore and find another book covering the same subject area that you can understand.

You might even consider asking your teacher or professor for recommendations. She will probably make your job of finding a readable text a lot easier. You may even score some brownie points for your seeming initiative (as long as you don't wonder aloud what caused her to select that torturous text in the first place!).

"Ron," I hear you grumbling, "what happened to the 'study smarter, not harder' bit? This can't possibly be a time saver. Heck, I'll bet the books don't even cover the subject in the same way, let alone follow the same sequence! I'll be stuck slogging through two books."

Possibly. But if you just don't get it, maybe it's because the author just doesn't know how to explain it. Maybe it's not your fault! Too many students have sweated, moaned, dropped classes, even changed majors because they thought they were dumb, when it's possible it's the darned textbook that's dense, not you. So instead of continuing to slog though the mire, find an expert who can actually write—they're out there—and learn what you need to. After finally gaining an understanding of the subject by reading this other text, you'll find much of the original textbook much easier to use... presuming you need it at all.

CHAPTER 2

READING WITH PURPOSE

Even if you consider yourself "not much of a reader," you read something each and every day: a magazine article, instructions for hooking up the DVD player, telephone messages tacked on the refrigerator, notes from your latest heartthrob.

Regardless of what you are reading, you have a purpose that dictates how you are going to read it—and you read different items in different ways. You wouldn't read the DVD player instructions as you would a novel any more than you'd read a magazine article in the same way as a grocery list. Without a purpose, you'd find yourself reading aimlessly and very inefficiently.

Unfortunately, many of the students I've talked to have not yet realized the importance of having a purpose for reading. Their lack of a reading purpose can be summed up by the proverb, "If you aim at nothing, you will hit the bull's-eye every time."

Before you can understand what you're reading—and remember it—you must know why you're reading it in the first place.

Defining Your Purpose for Reading

What is your purpose for reading? If the best answer you can come up with is, "Because my teacher said I had to," we need to uncover some better reasons. Reading a chapter just so you can say, "I finished my assignment" is relatively futile. You may as well put the book under a pillow and hope to absorb it by osmosis.

Unless you identify some purpose for reading, you will find yourself flipping the pages of your textbooks while seldom retaining anything more than the chapter titles.

According to reading experts, there are six fundamental purposes for reading:

1. To grasp a certain message.
2. To find important details.
3. To answer a specific question.
4. To evaluate what you are reading.
5. To apply what you are reading.
6. To be entertained.

Because reading with purpose is the first step toward improved comprehension, let me suggest some simple techniques you can use to identify a purpose for your textbook reading.

Find the Clues in Every Book

There is a group of special sections found in nearly all textbooks and technical materials (in fact, in almost all books except novels) that contain a wealth of information and can help you glean more from your reading. Becoming familiar with this data will enrich your reading experience and often make it easier. Here's what to look for.

The first page after the title page is usually the table of contents—a chapter-by-chapter list of the book's contents. Some are surprisingly detailed, listing every major point or topic covered in each chapter.

The first prose section (after the title page, table of contents, and, perhaps, an acknowledgments page), is the preface—a description of the information you will find in the book. Authors may also use the preface to point out unique aspects of their books.

The introduction may be in place of or in addition to the preface, written by the author or by some "name" the author has recruited to lend additional prestige to his or her work. Most introductions are an even more detailed overview of the book—chapter-by-chapter summaries are often included to give the reader a feel for the material to be covered.

Footnotes may be found throughout the text (a slightly elevated number following a sentence, quotation, or paragraph, e.g., "jim-dandy"[24]) and either explained at the bottom of the page on which they appear or in a special section at the back of the text. Footnotes may be used to cite sources of direct quotes or ideas and/or to further explain a point or add information outside of the text. You may make it a habit to ferret out sources cited for further reading.

If a text tends to use an alarmingly large number of terms with which you may not be familiar, the considerate author will include a glossary—essentially an abridged dictionary that defines all such terms.

The bibliography, usually at the end of the book, may include the source material the author used to research the textbook, a list of "recommended reading," or both. It is usually organized alphabetically by subject, making it easy for you to find more information on a specific topic.

Appendices containing supplementary data or examples relating to subject matter covered in the text may also appear in the back of the book.

The last thing in a book is usually the index, an alphabetical listing that references, by page number, every mention of a particular name, subject, and topic in the text.

Making it a habit to utilize all of these tools in your textbook can only make your studying easier.

Look for the Clues in Each Chapter

Every textbook offers some clues that will help you define a purpose for reading. Begin with a very quick overview of the assignment, looking for questions that you'd like answered. Consider the following elements of your reading assignment before you begin your reading.

Much like the headlines of a newspaper clue you into what the story is about, these elements will give insight into what the section or chapter is trying to communicate.

Chapter Heads and Subheads

Chapter titles and bold-faced subheads announce the detail about the main topic. And, in some textbooks, paragraph headings or bold-faced "lead-ins" announce that the author is about to provide finer details.

So start each reading assignment by going through the chapter, beginning to end, reading only the bold-faced heads and subheads.

For example, suppose you encountered the heading "The Fall of Communism" in your history textbook. You might use it to formulate the following questions:

1. *What* caused the fall of Communism?
2. *Who* caused it?
3. *When* did it fall?
4. *Why* did it fall?
5. *Where* did the fall occur?

As you read the chapter, you'll find yourself seeking answers to these questions. You now have a purpose!

Often you may find headings that contain words or terms you don't recognize. Seeking to define these terms or explain a concept should then define your purpose.

This process of headline reading takes only a few minutes, but it lays the groundwork for a more intelligent and efficient reading of the chapter. You'll have some idea of where the author is headed, which will give you a greater sense of what the most important details are and clarify where you should be concentrating your studying.

End-of-Chapter Summaries

If you read a mystery from start to finish, the way the author hopes you will, you're likely to get thrown off the scent by "red herrings" and other common detective novel devices. However, if you read the last page first, knowing the outcome will help you detect how the author constructed the novel and built an open-and-shut case for her master sleuth. You'd perceive a wealth of details about the eventually unmasked murderer that might have gone unnoticed had he been just another of the leading suspects.

Similarly, knowing what the author is driving at in a textbook will help you look for the important building blocks for his conclusions while you're reading.

It may not be fun to read a mystery novel this way, but when it comes to your textbooks, it will help you define your purpose for reading. And further, it will transform you into a much more active reader, making it less likely you'll doze off between the fall of Rome and the Black Plague.

Pictures, Graphs, and Charts

Most textbooks, particularly those in the sciences, will have charts, graphs, numerical tables, maps, and other illustrations. All too many students see these as fillers— padding to glance at and, just as quickly, forget.

If you're giving these charts and graphs short shrift, you're really shortchanging yourself. Be sure to observe how they supplement the text, what points they emphasize, and make note of these.

Highlighted Terms, Vocabulary, and Other Facts

In some textbooks, you'll discover that key terms and information are highlighted within the body text. (I don't mean highlighted by a previous student—consider such yellow-markered passages with caution!) To find the definitions of these terms or to find the application of facts may then be your purpose for reading.

Questions

Some textbook publishers use a format in which key points are emphasized by questions, either within the body or at the end of the chapter. If you read these questions before reading the chapter, you'll have a better idea of the material you should concentrate on.

If you begin your reading assignment by seeking out these heads, subheads, and other purpose-finding elements of the chapter, you'll have completed your prereading step. What is prereading? It is simply beginning your assigned reading by reviewing these clues and defining your purpose (or purposes) for reading.

I advise that you always preread every assignment! Why? Have you ever spent the better part of an evening plowing through an assignment only to finish with little or no understanding of what you just read? If the answer is yes, then you probably failed to preread it.

Reading Faster Without Speed Reading

While the heads, subheads, first sentences, and other author-provided hints we've talked about will help you get a quick read on what a chapter's about, some of the words in that chapter will help you concentrate on the important points and ignore the unimportant. Knowing when to speed up, slow down, ignore, or really concentrate will help you read both faster and more effectively.

When you see words such as "likewise," "in addition," "moreover," "furthermore," and the like, you should know that nothing new is being introduced. If you already know what's going on, speed up or skip what's coming entirely.

On the other hand, when you see words such as "on the other hand," "nevertheless," "however," "rather," "but," and their ilk, slow down—you're getting information that adds a new perspective or contradicts what you've just read.

Lastly, watch out for "payoff" words such as "to summarize," "in conclusion," "therefore," "consequently," "thus"— especially if you only have time to "hit the high points" of a chapter or you're reviewing for a test. Here's where the real meat is, where everything that went before is happily tied up in a nice bow and ribbon, a present that enables you to avoid having to unwrap the entire chapter.

Purpose Defines Reading Method

Typically, your purpose for reading dictates how you read. There are basically three types of reading we all do:

1. Quick reference reading focuses on seeking specific information that addresses a particular question or concern we might have.

2. Critical reading involves discerning ideas and concepts that require a thorough analysis.

3. Aesthetic, or pleasure reading, is what we do for sheer entertainment or to appreciate an author's style and ability.

As you define your purpose for reading, you will determine which method of reading is necessary to accomplish this purpose. In the following table are some examples of types of reading, why you might read them, and the method you should use:

Type	Purpose	Method
Newspaper advertisement	To locate best price for car	Quick reference
Magazine	To stay aware of current events	Quick reference
Self-help book	To learn to get along better with your family	Critical
Biology text	To prepare for an exam	Critical
New issue of *Rolling Stone*	To take your mind off biology!	Pleasure

If you're a good reader or desire to be one, you will always fit your reading method to your reading purpose; you have trained or are training yourself in a variety of reading skills; you have no problem switching your method to accommodate your purpose; and you are unsatisfied reading only one type of material.

A poor reader, on the other hand, reads everything the same way—doggedly plowing through his biology assignment, the newspaper, and a Stephen King novel…word by painful word. Reading with purpose is both foreign and foreboding to such a person, which makes it difficult for him to adapt a method of reading.

Become an Active Reader

Reading with purpose is as vital to your comprehension and retention as oxygen is to life. It is the cornerstone of active reading, reading that involves thinking—that process of engaging your mind and emotions in what the author is trying to communicate. Too many readers seek to absorb information passively as their eyes move across the page. The active reader involves him- or herself in receiving a message—a fact, an idea, an opinion—that is readily retained because he or she had a purpose.

Following are two passages. The first is adapted from *American Firsts* by Stephen Spignesi. The second is an excerpt from *Get Rich Slow* by Tama McAleese (Career Press, 2004). Preread each passage in order to determine a purpose for reading. Be sure to use the notes page following the passages to jot down questions that may have been raised through your preread, as well as your purpose.

Passage One

The polygraph (or "lie detector") measures physiological responses to questioning. Through various sensors and cuffs, the machine measures marked changes in blood pressure, heart rate, respiration, and perspiration, and interprets these changes to indicate that the person is being deceptive. The polygraph examiner, by law, cannot state that a person is lying. He or she can only report "Deception indicated," "No deception indicated," or "Inconclusive" for each of the examinee's responses.

The United States Supreme Court has ruled that polygraph results are inadmissible in court, writing, "there is simply no consensus that polygraph evidence is reliable…scientific field studies suggest the accuracy rate of the 'control question technique' polygraph is 'little better than could be obtained by the toss of a coin,' that is, 50 percent."

Some employers require a potential employee to submit to a lie detector test before being hired. Many job applicants do not know that they can legally decline to take the test and that they cannot be refused a job based on their unwillingness to take it. Many employees are also not aware that they can legally refuse to take a lie detector test, and that their employer cannot subsequently fire them. The only legally valid reason for an employer to demand a lie detector test of an employee is when there has been some type of embezzlement or other financial loss to the business, and the employer has reason to believe that the targeted employee was involved in the loss.

The reason polygraph results are not accepted in court is because polygraphs do not record lies; they record physical changes. Consider this scenario: You work for a company at which a computer was recently stolen from your department. You happened to see who stole it, but you had nothing to do with it, and the thief doesn't even know he was spotted. Your boss decides to polygraph everyone in the department, and when you are asked the question, "Did you steal the computer?" your blood pressure and pulse skyrocket because you do know who stole it. You answer "no" because you didn't steal it, but your body responds as if you did. In this scenario, the polygraph examiner would probably tell your boss that you were being deceptive when asked about the theft of the computer.

Your boss will probably then either fire you or make you submit to another polygraph test, which will likely turn out the same way, and then he'll fire you. You will have been branded a thief and lost your job simply because you got nervous about being asked a question about a stolen computer.

Is this fair? Of course not, and that is why polygraph results are not accepted in court.

There are books and websites devoted to teaching people how to beat a lie detector test. Some common tactics include taking a sedative before the test, placing a tack in your shoe and then stepping on it after each question, and placing deodorant on your fingertips. I have also heard of people who lie in response to every question—even "control" questions like their name, address, or gender—so the examiner cannot get a base response reading.

John Larson's invention has been the source of endless controversy, and much of the ongoing debate has been about whether or not Larson's basic postulate—that people get nervous when they lie—is true. As we all know, some people are incredibly convincing liars. They can tell you that the sky is green so persuasively that they have you looking up to confirm it's still blue.

Individuals' responses to being questioned are diverse and unpredictable. This unavoidable fact is why the Supreme Court has (wisely) rejected allowing polygraph results as valid evidence in trials.

Passage Two

Ask most real estate agents, brokers, or lending institutions when the best time to buy a house is and their response will usually be, "Now." If interest rates are low, buy before they go up. If rates are soaring, buy now before they go higher. Can't afford a reasonable down payment? That's what creative financing, private mortgage insurance (PMI), jumbo mortgages, and government subsidies are for. Don't know how long you will stay in an area? Buy that house now and count your profits when you move, or keep it and rent it out for a steady monthly income. Haven't saved up a reasonable down payment? Lenders will loan you more. Can't fit the hefty monthly payments into your budget? Then spread them out over a 30-year indentured servant plan, which will give you lower payments along with a life sentence of payments. Thinking about renting for a while first? You're throwing money down the drain. You don't get anything back when you rent. Look at all the equity that you could be building up in a home instead of making a landlord rich.

The real estate industry makes its money by moving real estate around from seller to buyer. It profits from pitching the advantages of home-buying. When money is deposited into a bank, it must be loaned out as soon as possible. What can the average American do with a big chunk of loaned money? He or she can buy real estate. So, the lender benefits by extolling the virtues of home ownership.

The federal government must find ways of keeping the country expanding and workers employed. The nation's economic health is closely tied to new housing construction and existing housing sales. So Uncle Sam also has a vested interest in encouraging you to purchase the American dream.

The building industry uses the real estate industry as a middleman to turn over its housing inventory. This feeds the banking industry, which then turns to the government for guaranteed backing (something the government gets from us by selling home mortgages to investors). The insurance agent, the furniture store vendor, the county tax assessor, and the landscaper are just a few of the businesses that benefit when you commit to a home mortgage.

Homeowners are pitched so-called benefits from mortgage interest tax deductions, tax deferrals on profits from the price appreciation of their house over time, VA (Veterans Administration) and FHA (Federal Housing Authority) federally subsidized mortgage loan programs for homebuyers with little down payment. GNMA (Government National Mortgage Association, or "Ginnie Mae"), FNMA (Federal National Mortgage Association, or "Fannie Mae"), and FMAC (Federal Agricultural Mortgage Corporation, or "Farmer Mac") are lenders willing to guarantee mortgage funds back to the original lender should a homeowner default. Community rehab loans and a plump $250,000 profit per-person tax-free exclusion every two years if the house sold is your primary residence usually clinches the home sale. The homebuying industry has an expensive and powerful agenda designed to keep its bottom line healthy. You often hear the attractive spiel: With a home, you have status; an inflation hedge; tax deductions; tax-sheltered growth; a sound, low-risk investment; increased home value through improvements; a safe investment over time; easy purchase plans; U.S. government assistance; marketability; the pride of ownership; greater family privacy; control over the roof over your head; and a proper environment to raise a family. After all, this is the American way.

But compare real estate to a bank CD as an alternative investment. Can you sell your home as fast as you can cash in a CD? Does a personal residence generate monthly or quarterly income, or any other type of guaranteed interest? Can you purchase a home as cheaply as a CD? Is the principal in your home guaranteed like the backing behind a bank CD?

There are greater risks to owning real estate than meets the eye. What about liquidity? Are you guaranteed a return on every dollar you sink into your home at sale time? The costs associated with buying and selling, and improvements and maintenance over time must be subtracted from any ultimate profits.

What if your house loses value because markets decline? Real estate doesn't always go up in price. Some homeowners have suffered major losses by buying at the top of their regional property markets. Profits they were depending on never materialized.

A CD is protected from loss of principal by an agency of the U.S. government. Can you move at a moment's notice like you can redeem your bank CD? When you rent, you are bound to stay only under the terms of your lease. The most you could lose is generally your security deposit. Do you need a job, good credit, a mortgage loan, and the promise of continued employment to buy a CD like you do to buy a house? The costs of borrowed money over the life of the mortgage are not even whispered in hallowed mortgage departments.

Can your real estate keep pace with the return on a bank CD? Probably not. On a conventional 20-year loan, you will fork over twice the amount of loan you borrowed. Over 30 years, you will pay back nearly three times the original debt. A home would have to double in price every 20 years just to keep up with that cost alone. For a 30-year loan, you would have to net three times the price you paid.

The average home cannot keep pace with a bank CD when you include the costs of ownership. Even if your home appreciates handsomely over time, there are other expenses to consider. You don't have to buy fire or theft insurance for your CD, pay property taxes or assessments or buying and selling costs, make improvements, bring your CD up to code, worry about its safety during tornado or hurricane season, or spend more money to maintain it.

Your home may be the priciest purchase you ever make. But generally it won't be listed among the top-10 smartest investments. It may even rank as one of the worst. Think of a home as a roof over your head, a place to hang your hat, and a lifestyle decision, and not as a shrewd financial investment.

Your Notes

What clues did you find that helped you define a purpose for
reading each passage?

_____

_____

_____

_____

_____

_____

_____

_____

What purpose or purposes did you determine for reading
each passage?

_____

_____

_____

_____

_____

_____

_____

_____

What method, based on your purpose, did you use to read
each passage?

_____

_____

_____

_____

_____

_____

_____

CHAPTER 3

FINDING THE MAIN IDEA

I n all good writing there is a controlling thesis or message that connects all of the specific details and facts. This concept or idea is usually expressed as a generalization that summarizes the entire text.

Good comprehension results when you are able to grasp this main message, even if you sometimes forget some of the details. When you understand the intent, you have a context in which to evaluate the reasoning, the attitude, and whether the evidence cited really is supportive of the conclusions drawn.

An obsession for facts can obscure the "big picture," giving you an understanding of the trees but no concept of the forest. How many of you have spent hours studying for an important exam, collecting dates, names, terms, and formulas, but failed to ferret out the main idea, the underlying concept that is composed of these facts?

In longer, more involved readings, many messages are combined to form a chain of thought, which, in turn, may or may not communicate one thesis or idea.

Your ability to capture this chain of thought determines your level of comprehension—and what you retain.

Dissecting Your Reading Assignment

To succeed in identifying the main idea in any reading assignment, you must learn to use these helpful tools:

1. The topic sentence of a paragraph.

2. Summary sentences.

3. Supporting sentences.

4. Transitional statements.

As you learn to dissect your reading assignment paragraph by paragraph, identifying its many parts and their functions, you'll grasp the main idea much more quickly—and remember it much longer.

Recognizing a Topic Sentence

Every paragraph has a topic sentence—the sentence that summarizes what the paragraph is about. Even if a paragraph does not have such a clearly stated sentence, it can be implied or inferred from what is written.

Generally, the topic sentence is the first or last sentence of a paragraph—the one statement that announces, "Here's what this paragraph is all about!"

When the topic sentence is obscured or hidden, you may need to utilize two simple exercises to uncover it:

1. Pretend you're a headline writer for your local newspaper and write a headline for the paragraph you just read.

2. Write a five-word summary describing what the paragraph is about.

Exercise: Identifying a Topic Sentence

Write a headline or five-word summary for each of the following paragraphs:

Mary Phelps Jacob invented the brassiere when she needed something to wear beneath a gown and none of the existing undergarments of the time gave her the support the garment required. Women wore corsets back then, and they were bulky, uncomfortable, and did not work for many types of dresses. In Mary's case, the sheer gown she had bought had a plunging neckline and the whalebone inserts of her corsets were visible. After a little thought, Mary designed the first bra using nothing but two silk handkerchiefs and some pink ribbon. She fashioned two cups out of the handkerchiefs, used the ribbon to tie them and, voila, no more corsets!

Jazz is a musical feast, and its recipe includes African-American gospel spirituals, blues, ragtime, and other musical forms popularized and remade by American musicians. The earliest pioneers of jazz were the New Orleans Dixieland musicians who taught themselves to play, but who could not read or write music. They would turn beloved old favorites like "When the Saints Come Marching In" and "The Battle Hymn of the Republic" into rollicking, freeform musical epics.

Early versions of sewing machines were created in England and France, but they were completely unworkable as commercial machines. Thomas Saint's machine, for example, designed in 1790 to sew leather, was never even built. Barthelmy Thimonnier invented a machine in France in the late 1820s that sewed a chain stitch using a crocheting needle. He enjoyed some success with the machine sewing soldier's uniforms for the French Army, but his shop and machines were destroyed by rampaging tailors who believed that Thimonnier was set on putting them out of business and that any machines designed to replace human labor were sinful.

You can begin your analysis by turning, once again, to our helpful questions. Is the passage written to address one of the questions?

1. **Who?** The paragraph focuses on a particular person or group of people. The topic sentence tells you who this is.

2. **When?** The paragraph is primarily concerned with time. The topic sentence may even begin with the word "when."

3. **Where?** The paragraph is oriented around a particular place or location. The topic sentence states where you are reading about.

4. **Why?** A paragraph that states reasons for some belief or happening usually addresses this question. The topic sentence answers why something is true or why an event happened.

5. **How?** The paragraph identifies the way something works or the means by which something is done. The topic sentence explains the how of what is described.

You will notice that I didn't include the question "What?" in this list. This is not an oversight. "What?" addresses such a broad range of possibilities that asking this question will not necessarily lead you to the topic sentence.

The best test to determine whether you have identified the topic sentence is to rephrase it as a question. If the paragraph answers the question that you've framed, you've found the topic sentence.

Summary, Support, or Transitional?

Another technique that will lead you to the topic sentence is to identify what purpose other sentences in the paragraph serve—kind of a process of elimination.

Generally, sentences can be characterized as summary, support, or transitional.

Summary sentences state a general idea or concept. As a rule, a topic sentence is a summary sentence—a concise yet inclusive statement that expresses the general intent of the paragraph. (By definition, the topic sentence is never a support sentence.)

Support sentences provide the specific details and facts that give credibility to the author's points of view. They give examples, explain arguments, offer evidence, or attempt to prove something as true or false. They are not meant to state generally what the author wants to communicate—they are intended to be specific, not conceptual, in nature.

Transitional sentences move the author from one point to another. They may be viewed as bridges connecting the paragraphs in a text, suggesting the relationship between what you just finished reading and what you are about to read. Good readers are attuned to the signals such sentences provide—they are buzzers that scream, "This is what you are going to find out next!"

Transitional sentences may also alert you to what you should have just learned. Unlike support sentences, transitional sentences provide invaluable and direct clues to identifying the topic sentence.

Some Examples of Transitional Signals

Any sentence that continues a progression of thought or succession of concepts is a transitional sentence. Such a sentence may begin with a word such as "first," "next," "finally," or "then," and indicate the before/after connection between changes, improvements, or alterations.

Transitional sentences that begin in this way should raise these questions in your mind:

1. Do I know what the previous examples were?
2. What additional example am I about to learn?
3. What was the situation prior to the change?

Other transition statements suggest a change in argument or thought or an exception to a rule. These will generally be introduced by words like "but," "although," "though," "rather," "however," or similar conjunctions that suggest an opposing thought.

Such words ought to raise these questions:

1. What is the gist of the argument I just read?
2. What will the argument I am about to read state?
3. To what rule is the author offering an exception?

In your effort to improve your reading, developing the ability to recognize the contrast between general, inclusive words and statements (summary sentences) and specific, detail-oriented sentences (transitional or support sentences) is paramount.

Taking Notes

The final step toward grasping and retaining the main idea of any paragraph is taking notes. There are several traditional methods students employ—outlining, highlighting, mapping, and drawing concept trees.

An exhaustive review of all these methods is not within the scope of this particular book, but for a complete discussion of note-taking techniques, be sure to read *Surefire Tips to Improve Your Organization Skills,* another of the books in my this series.

Whichever method you employ to retain the main idea, focus on the topic sentences, not on the specific details.

If you are a highlighter—you enjoy coloring textbooks with fluorescent markers—you will want to assign one color that you will always use to highlight topic sentences. Avoid what too many students do—highlighting virtually every paragraph. This practice will just extend your review time considerably—you'll find yourself rereading instead of reviewing.

If you utilize outlining or mapping (diagramming what you read rather than spending time worrying about Roman numerals and whether to use lowercase letters or uppercase letters on certain lines), you will find that your time will best be spent writing five-word summaries of the topic sentences.

If you find yourself getting bogged down in details and specifics, you are wasting valuable time. Again, writers are using these details to communicate their concepts—they are not necessarily to be remembered.

Read the following passages, seeking out the topic sentences. Then summarize the main idea or ideas in five-word phrases. (The first two are adapted from *American Firsts* by Stephen Spignesi, which, as you probably have guessed, is a favorite of mine; the last from *Why Women Earn Less* by Mikelann R. Valterra [Career Press, 2004].)

Passage One

American Alexander Graham Bell did not invent the telephone; Italian-American Antonio Meucci did. On June 15, 2002, the United States Congress officially recognized Meucci as the true inventor of the telephone. Many of you may know that Bell received the patent for a telephonic device mere hours before a patent for a similar device by an inventor named Elisha Gray was filed. What many of you probably do not know is that it has now been proven that Bell probably stole the idea for the telephone from designs and drawings by Antonio Meucci that were stored in the laboratory where Bell worked. The United States Supreme Court annulled Bell's patent in 1887 on the grounds of fraud and misrepresentation.

The telephone patent is considered today to be the most valuable patent ever issued by the U.S. government. Meucci was born in Florence, Italy, in 1807 and emigrated to America in 1845. Between 1850 and 1862, Meucci developed at least 30 different models of working telephones. (The German inventor Philip Reis, who has sometimes also been credited as being the true inventor of the telephone, invented a voice-transmitting device in 1861, more than a decade after Meucci's earliest models.)

However, Meucci was too poor to pay the fees required to patent his inventions (around $250), and he had to settle for a document called a Caveat, which was a formal legal notice that stated that he had invented the telephone. The caveat was meant to be temporary until official patent papers could be acquired, but Meucci did not even have the money to renew the caveat. In 1874, he turned over some of his models to the vice president of Western Union Telegraphs, and, two years later, read in the newspaper that Alexander Graham Bell (who, remember, had been working at the Western Union Labs), had patented a telephone and taken full credit for its invention. Even though this patent was annulled, Meucci never profited from his invention and he died poor in 1889.

Passage Two

Rituals have arisen surrounding the game of Monopoly. Some people will only play if they are the thimble, or the top hat. Some will only target certain properties to purchase. Some will take a drink every time they pay rent. And then there's naked Monopoly...but we won't go there.

Monopoly is the world's best-selling board game. Yes, in this age of computer and video games and astonishingly high-tech handheld games, the defiantly low-tech Monopoly is still the king. Who invented the game of Monopoly? History accepts Charles Darrow as the inventor because he was the one who went to Parker Brothers with the idea, he was the one from whom they bought the rights, and he was the one who became a millionaire from Monopoly royalties.

However, there is compelling evidence that Darrow was taught the game by a woman who had been playing something she had invented, called The Landlord's Game, for years. The Landlord's Game was very similar to today's Monopoly except that the goal was not to acquire property, but rather to denigrate property ownership and landlords.

The story told by those in the Darrow camp is that Darrow came up with the idea for Monopoly when he was unemployed during the Great Depression. He nostalgically sketched out the streets of his childhood hometown of Atlantic City, New Jersey, and eventually developed the idea of buying and selling property as the "play" of the game. Supposedly, his friends and neighbors loved the game and would spend evenings playing it at the Darrow home. Darrow began making copies of the game board and rules and selling them for four dollars apiece. He also began offering it to stores in Philadelphia.

The game's burgeoning popularity spurred Darrow to offer it to Parker Brothers, who turned it down because it took too long to play and because they said it was too complicated.

Darrow was not discouraged, though, and continued to market the game on his own.

How did it eventually end up a Parker Brothers game after Parker Brothers rejected it? A friend of one of George Parker's daughters bought one of Darrow's games and recommended it to Parker's daughter Sally. This time, Parker Brothers sought out Darrow and bought the rights to the game.

This story is the "official" version. There have been several lawsuits, however, regarding the true genesis of the game, and Parker Brothers has paid out cash settlements to people who have shown that Darrow likely did not create Monopoly on his own.

Passage Three

Many women chronically earn less than they could, and are tired and frustrated at their apparent inability to increase their earnings. This pattern of not making enough money is called "underearning," and is a tragic waste of potential and possibility in the lives of thousands of women. Underearning happens when you repeatedly (and consistently) make less than you need or than would be helpful to you, usually despite your desire to make more money. Put another way: An underearner is someone who doesn't get paid as much as might be expected, given her experience, education, and training.

Underearning takes on many forms and can be as creative and varied as the underearner. Those on a salary may have a hard time asking for that long over-due raise, while those who are self-employed might find it difficult to raise their fees. Sometimes people give their time away by under-billing. Others under-earn by using all their energy for volunteer activities, and in the process give away their skills and experience. And some people underearn by failing to market them-selves, whether or not they are self-employed.

Some of these practices are part of everyday life, and are so common that most women do not understand how their behavior limits their earning potential. Also, underearning can result from what one doesn't do, which makes it more easily unnoticed, ignored, or forgotten. But the end result is the same: when women undersell themselves, the price they pay is very high. Millions of women underearn—yet have no idea they are doing so.

During the course of a working lifetime, this chronic underselling results in the loss of what most of us would consider a small fortune. In fact, current research shows that the average 25-year-old woman will earn $523,000 less than her male counterpart over the next 40 years, according to the Institute of Women's Policy Research. Imagine—more than half a million dollars lost, never to be recouped! That's the bad news. The good news is that many of the causes of underearning can be eliminated, and you have the power to make that happen, though you may not yet realize it.

It is possible to make more money. But in order to do so, you must first learn how to recognize your own underearning, and to understand the issues that motivate your behavior. Only then can you develop a solid, workable plan to reverse the pattern of selling yourself short.

So how did you do taking notes on these three examples? I didn't always keep my summaries to five words, but I distilled the main ideas to the fewest words I could.

Nor did I always write one summary statement per paragraph—just what was needed to capture the main idea or ideas from each paragraph.

CHAPTER 4

GATHERING THE FACTS

"Now, what I want is facts. Teach these boys and girls nothing but facts.
Facts alone are wanted in life. Plant nothing else, and root out
everything else. You can only form the minds of reasoning animals
upon facts: nothing else will ever be of any service to them.
This is the principle on which I bring up my own children,
and this is the principle on which I bring up these children.
Stick to facts, sir!"

—Charles Dickens, *Hard Times*

While such an approach is not the only ingredient for scholastic success, you'll find that the vast majority of your assigned reading requires a thorough recall of the facts.

In the previous chapter, we discussed the "forest"—the main idea. In this chapter, we will concentrate on "the trees"— how to read to gather facts, the specific details that support and develop the author's main point.

Facts: Building Blocks for Ideas

Facts are the building blocks that give credibility to concepts and ideas. Your ability to gather and assimilate these facts will dramatically enhance your success at remembering what the author wanted to communicate.

If, however, you spend so much time studying the trees that you lose sight of the forest, your reading effectiveness will be limited. You must learn to discern what facts are salient to your understanding, and which ones to leave for the next Trivial Pursuit update.

If you are trying to identify your purpose for reading this chapter, it's threefold:

1. To develop the skill of scanning a text for facts as quickly as possible.

2. To distinguish between an important detail and a trivial one.

3. To learn how to skim text—reading and absorbing its essence, even when you're not looking for anything in particular.

Deciphering the Message

The author of any kind of writing should have something to say, a message to communicate.

Unfortunately, such messages are often lost in the glut of verbiage many authors use to "dress up" their basic point. It's your job to rake through the mess and get to the heart of the text.

You need to approach each reading assignment with the mind-set of Sherlock Holmes: There is a mystery to be solved, and you are the master detective. The goal is to figure out what the text is trying to communicate—regardless of how deeply it is buried in the quagmire of convoluted language.

What Is the Message?

The first step in any good investigation is to collect all of the clues. What are the facts? By spending a few minutes of your time discerning these concrete facts, you will be far better equipped to digest what it is the author is trying to communicate.

But how do you extract the facts when they appear to be hidden in an impenetrable forest of words? You may need a little help—from "who-what-when-where-why-and-how." It seems that the facts readily sally forth when these six trusty questions are called upon the scene.

Exercise: Read the following excerpt (from *Homework Helpers: Biology* by Matthew Distefano, Career Press, 2004), keeping those six words in mind, then answer the questions that follow.

The earliest development of the microscope took place a long time after people had discovered the magnifying power of lenses. A container of water, a bead of glass, or a gemstone can all magnify objects to some degree and can be considered early lenses. Roger Bacon (1214–1294) is given credit for introducing the magnifying lens as eye glasses, or spectacles, as they were known during his time, in 1268. This is probably the first recorded time a magnifying glass was used to support human eyesight.

It would take several hundred years before these glass lenses were used to make distant objects appear closer or small objects appear bigger. The invention of the telescope was in 1608 by a Dutch lens maker named Hans Lippershey. The microscope was probably created a few years earlier, around 1597, by Zaccharias Jansseen and his son Han, who were also Dutch lens makers. This father-and-son combo created the earliest documented compound microscope by focusing light through two lenses. Robert Hooke would later refine the structure of the compound microscope.

Anton van Leeuwenhoek (1632–1723), a naturalist and lens maker, constructed a very powerful lens to view small objects. Van Leeuwenhoek created large single lens microscopes that could magnify objects up to 270X their normal size. With these lenses, he saw small objects that had never been seen by human eyes before, such as bacterial cells, protozoa, and blood and yeast cells.

Robert Hooke (1635–1703), a physicist by trade, refined the structure of the compound microscope. As mentioned earlier, a compound microscope is a microscope where the object is now viewed through two lenses, instead of just one. Hooke is credited with coining the word "cell," when he described the many small, interconnected boxes he saw under the microscope while looking at a piece of cork. Cork is made from tree bark, so it consists of dead plant cells. Hooke, although not known to him at the time, was viewing these dead plant cells.

In 1831, Robert Brown, a botanist, was the first to describe the dark, circular object found at the center of all plant cells as a nucleus.

In 1838, Matthias Schleiden, a botanist, and Theodor Schwann, a zoologist, concluded that all living things are made of cells, and in 1855, Rudolph Virchow added that all cells arise only from other living cells. The work of these three scientists led to what is today known as the cell theory.

Questions

1. Who first described the nucleus?
   - A. Rudolph Virchow
   - B. Matthias Schleiden
   - C. Theodor Schwann
   - D. None of the above

2. About how many times could van Leeuwenhoek's lens magnify objects?
   - A. 10
   - B. 100
   - C. 200
   - D. 300

3. In what century was the microscope probably invented?
   - A. 15th
   - B. 16th
   - C. 17th
   - D. 18th

4. In what century was the magnifying lens first used in eyeglasses?
    A. 12th
    B. 13th
    C. 15th
    D. 17th

5. Who invented the telescope?
    A. Robert Brown
    B. Anton van Leeuwenhoek
    C. Robert Hooke
    D. Hans Lippershey

In the preceding exercise, you should have quickly read through the text and been able to answer all five questions. If it took you more than three minutes to do so, you spent too much time. You were reading only to answer "who?", "what?", "when?", "where?", "why?", and "how?" Your purpose was to get to the facts, nothing more.

Scanning, Skimming, Reading, Remembering

Most everyone I know confuses skim and scan. Let me set the record straight. Skim is to read quickly and superficially. Scan is to read carefully but for a specific item. So when you skim a reading selection, you are reading it in its entirety, though you're only hitting the "highlights."

When you scan a selection, you are reading it in detail but only until you find what you're looking for. Scanning is the technique we all employ when using the phone book—unless, of course, you're in the habit of reading every name in the book to find the one you're looking for. When you scan, your eyes do not look at every word, read every sentence, or think about every paragraph. Instead, they rapidly move across the page to find just what you are looking for and then read that carefully.

Scanning is the fastest reading rate of all—although you are reading in detail, you are not seeking to comprehend or remember anything that you see until you find the bit of information you're looking for.

When I was in college, I would begin any assignment by reading the first sentence of every paragraph and trying to answer the questions at the chapter's end. If this did not give me a pretty good idea of the content and important details of that chapter, then—and only then—would I read it more thoroughly.

I'm sure this method of skimming for the facts saved me countless hours of time (and boredom).

Ask First, Then Look

When skimming for detail, you will often have a particular question, date, or fact to find. You should approach the text much like the dictionary—knowing the word, you just scan the pages to find its definition. If you must answer a specific question or read about a historic figure, you simply find a source—book, magazine, encyclopedia, or website—and quickly scan the text for the answer or person.

You probably are assigned a lot of reading that can be accomplished by skimming for facts. By establishing the questions you want answered before you begin to read, you can quickly browse through the material, extracting only the information you need.

Let's say you're reading a science book with the goal of identifying the function of a cell's nucleus. You can breeze through the section that gives the parts of the cell. You can skim the description of what cells do. You already know what you're looking for—and there it is in the section that talks about what each cell part does. Now you can start to read.

By identifying the questions you wanted to answer (a.k.a. your purpose) in advance, you would be able to skim the chapter and answer your questions in a lot less time than it would have taken to painstakingly read every word.

As a general rule, if you are reading textbook material word for word, you probably are wasting quite a bit of your study time. Good readers are able to discern what they should read in this manner and what they can afford to skim. When trying to simply gather detail and facts, skimming a text is a simple and very important shortcut.

Alternatively, your ability to skim a chapter—even something you need to read more critically—will enable you to develop a general sense of what the chapter is about and how thoroughly it needs to be read.

Exercise: Answer the following questions by skimming the paragraph that follows:

1. How many miles of coastline does Brazil have?
2. Which two South American countries do not border Brazil?
3. Which river is Brazil home to?

The largest country in South America is also the fifth largest country in the world. The Republic of Brazil is a vast land covering more than 3.3 million square miles—nearly half of the continent—with 4,600 miles of coastline looking out into the Atlantic Ocean. Brazil borders every country in South America except for Chile and Ecuador. This huge nation is home to a variety of climates and natural attractions, including immense rainforests and the world's largest river, the Amazon.

If this were part of your assigned reading, you would be finished when you had answered the questions. "But I didn't read it," you protest. Can you write a one-sentence summary of the paragraph? If you can, and you answered the questions correctly, then you know all you need to.

Skimming, or prereading, is a valuable step even if you aren't seeking specific facts. When skimming for a general overview, there's a very simple procedure to follow:

1. If there is a title or heading, rephrase it as a question. This will be your purpose for reading.

2. Examine all the subheadings, illustrations, and graphics, as these will help you identify the significant matter within the text.

3. Read thoroughly the introductory paragraphs, the summary, and any questions at the chapter's end.

4. Read the first sentence of every paragraph. As we found in Chapter 3, this is generally where the main idea of a text is found.

5. Evaluate what you have gained from this process: Can you answer the questions at the end of the chapter? Could you intelligently participate in a class discussion of the material?

6. Write a brief summary that encapsulates what you have learned from your skimming.

7. Based on this evaluation, decide whether a more thorough reading is required.

Exercise: Let's see how well you can skim for an overview, rather than for specific facts. Read the following two passages, then follow the seven steps outlined previously for each. The first is from *Hollywood Urban Legends* (New Page Books, 2001) by movie reviewer Roger Ebert's erstwhile partner, Richard Roeper. The second is from William's Weir's description of the battle of Hattin in 1187 A.D. in *50 Battles That Changed the World* (New Page Books, 2001).

Passage One

What a group of misfit castaways they truly were, from the fat guy who always thought he was in charge to the old crank to the sexy young babes to the unathletic guy who couldn't do anything right. No, I'm not talking about the first season of *Survivor,* I'm talking about *Gilligan's Island*.

Now, you might think of *G.I.* (as Tina Louise has always insisted on calling it in interviews because she can't bear to say the name "Gilligan" anymore) as nothing more than an astoundingly idiotic, stupid sitcom with no redeeming values—a brainless exercise in lamebrained humor that will play forever in Rerun Hell.

Well, you're probably right. But there are those who believe that *Gilligan's Island* is so much more complex than that. The show's creator, Sherwood Schwartz, is a learned and sophisticated man who always felt guilty about going into television, because he knew his creative genius could have been put to better use in another field, like rocket science or plastics. Deep down, Schwartz wanted to give the world TV programs that would educate us, that would tell us something about the human condition, that would elevate the human spirit—but the powers-that-be at the network level didn't want to hear that sort of nonsense. They wanted funny hits—commercially viable pap that could be used to sell dishwashing detergent and new cars to the masses. In other words, they wanted *Gilligan's Island*.

Little did the execs at CBS know that Schwartz played a trick of sorts with *Gilligan's Island* by giving it a subliminal second life that existed as a running social commentary about the state of the world. Not even the writers or cast members knew about this, but the truth is, they each represented one of the seven deadly sins!

1. Ginger, with her Marilyn Monroe voice and her plunging neckline gowns, was Lust.

2. Mary Ann, who could never be as sexy as Ginger, was Envy.

3. The Professor, who could construct a telescope from a coconut shell and bragged about knowing a little bit about everything, was Pride.

4. Mr. Howell, the millionaire, was Greed.

5. Mrs. Howell, who treated the other castaways like they were her servants and never did anything herself, was Sloth.

6. The Skipper, with his insatiable appetite, was Gluttony.

7. The Skipper was also Anger, for constantly losing his temper and hitting Gilligan with his hat.

And that leaves the deceptively benign Gilligan, who was Satan himself. *Gilligan's Island* is actually Hell! He keeps the others there through one foul-up after another. Week after week, the castaways are allowed to glimpse a ray of hope that they'll be able to get off the island, but it's all a mirage. They never realize that they're doomed to spend all eternity there—courtesy of Gilligan, who always wears red, the most devilish of colors.

Gilligan's Island as a metaphor for Hell is also Schwartz's way of admitting his own existence was hellish. Just as the castaways were trapped on that island, Schwartz was trapped in the mindless world of TV sitcoms, doomed to spend his professional life wallowing in shallow inanity. Pretty deep lagoon we're wading in, eh? Academic journals and Internet philosophers have delighted in advancing the "Seven Deadly Sins" theory of *Gilligan's Island,* and in later years, Schwartz himself has not discouraged such thought.

Passage Two

"So formidable is the charge of the Frankish cavalry with their broadsword, lance, and shield, that it is best to decline a pitched battle with them until you have put all the chances on your own side."

So advised the Byzantine emperor, Leo the Wise. Leo was thinking of the knights of the Carolingian Empire, but the techniques of Charlemagne's knights had been adopted all over Europe when the Crusades began. Still, perhaps because the first Crusaders were overwhelmingly French or Norman, to Byzantines and Muslims alike, all Westerners were "Franks." And Leo's advice was still sound.

War in Europe—a moist mass of peninsulas and islands, covered with forests and broken up by rivers and mountains—meant fighting at close quarters. Knights were encased in heavy mail, and foot soldiers wore as much armor as they could afford. Often the knight's huge charger, or destrier, was also armored. The destrier's saddle let the knight put all his weight and his horse's weight behind a lance thrust. The lance and the sword were the Western knight's only weapons, the charge his only tactic.

Horsemen of the steppes, unhampered by woods or many rivers, covered wide areas in their skirmishing. They depended mostly on the bow and usually charged only after their foes had been thoroughly softened up by archery. Asian tactics left little room for infantry, except in sieges.

The Frankish footmen, who had beaten the Romans, Goths, Vandals, Huns, and Arabs for centuries, had not forgotten how to fight. They were armed with spears, shields, and a new weapon: the recently reinvented crossbow.

Anna Comnena, a Byzantine princess, described the device she saw in the hands of the first Crusaders: "It is a weapon unknown to Greeks and to the Barbarians. This terrible weapon is not worked by drawing its cord with the right hand, and holding it with the left hand. The user rests both his feet against the bow, whilst he strains at the bow with the full force of his arms... When the cord is released, the arrow leaves the groove with a force against which nothing is proof. It not only penetrates a buckler, but also pierces the man and his armour through and through."

The Crusaders' military system was based on the close coordination of crossbowmen, infantry spearmen, and heavily armored knights. The disciplined spearmen kept the Turkish horse archers away from the knights, who led their destriers until they were ready to fight. Between every two spearmen was a crossbow-man who shot down Saracens before they could get close enough to hit anything with their bows. If the frustrated Muslims tried to break through the Christian lines with a mass attack, the infantry opened its ranks and the mounted knights charged. As at Marathon, the Westerners had heavier armor and carried longer spears. Unless there was an enormous imbalance of numbers the Muslims always lost.

While it may not be evident at first, you'll soon see how skimming can save you a lot of reading time. Even if a more in-depth reading is necessary, you will find that by having gone through this process, you will have developed the kind of skeletal framework that will make your further reading faster, easier, and more meaningful. And if all you need is "Just the facts, ma'am," your ability to scan a selection, chapter, or book will save you minutes, if not hours, every week.

Whether you're skimming or scanning, you will have equipped yourself with the ability to better digest whatever the author is trying to communicate.

CHAPTER 5

THE CHALLENGE OF TECHNICAL TEXTS

You've already learned a lot of ways to improve your reading. It's time to examine the unique challenges posed by highly technical texts. Physics, trigonometry, chemistry, calculus—you know, subjects that three-fourths of all students avoid like the plague. Even those students who manage to do well in such subjects wouldn't dare call them "Mickey Mouse" courses.

More than any other kind of reading, these subjects demand a logical, organized approach and a step-by-step reading method.

And they require a detection of the text's organizational devices.

Developing the skill to identify the basic sequence of the text will enable you to follow the progression of thought, a progression that is vital to your comprehension and retention.

Why? In most technical writing, each concept is a like a building block of understanding—if you don't understand a particular section or concept, you won't be able to understand the next section either.

Most technical books are saturated with ideas, terms, formulas, and theories. The chapters are dense with information, compressing a great wealth of ideas into a small space. They demand to be read very carefully.

In order to get as much as possible from such reading assignments, you can take advantage of some devices to make sense of the organization. Here are five basics to watch for:

1. Definitions and terms.

2. Examples.

3. Classifications and listings.

4. Comparison and contrast.

5. Cause-effect relationships.

As you read any text, but certainly a highly specialized one, identifying these devices will help you grasp the main idea, as well as any details that are essential to your thorough understanding of the material.

Definitions and Terms

In reading any specialized text, you must begin at the beginning—understanding the terms particular to that discipline. Familiar, everyday words have very precise definitions in technical writing.

What do I mean? Take the word nice. You may compliment your friend's new sweater, telling her it's nice, meaning attractive. You may find that the new chemistry teacher is nice, meaning he doesn't give too much homework. And when your friend uses the word nice to describe the blind date she's set up for you, it may mean something completely different—and insidious.

Everyday words can have a variety of meanings, some of them even contradictory, depending on the context in which they're used.

In contrast, in the sciences, terminology has fixed and specific meanings. For example, the definition of elasticity— "the ability of a solid to regain its shape after a deforming force has been applied"—is the same in Bangkok or Brooklyn. Such exact terminology enables scientists to communicate with the precision their discipline requires.

Definitions may vary in length. One term may require a one sentence definition; others merit entire paragraphs. Some may even need a whole chapter to accurately communicate the definition.

Look for key words that indicate specific mathematical operations. You need to add when you see words such as "increased by," "combined," "together," "sum," or "total of;" subtract when you see "decreased by," "minus," "less," "difference;" multiply when you see "product," "increased," "by a factor of," and "times;" and divide when you see "per," "ratio," "quotient," or "percent."

Examples

A second communication tool is the example. Authors use examples as bridges between abstract principles and concrete illustrations. These examples are essential to your ability to comprehend intricate and complicated theories.

Unlike other writing, technical writing places a very high premium on brevity. Economizing words is the key to covering a large volume of knowledge in a relatively small space. Few technical texts or articles include anecdotal matter or chatty stories on the author's experiences.

This fact challenges the reader to pay particular attention to the examples that are included. Why? Technical writing often is filled with new or foreign ideas—many of which are not readily digestible. They are difficult in part because they are abstract. Examples work to clarify these concepts, hopefully in terms that are more easily understood.

For example, it may be difficult for you to make sense of the definition of symbiosis—"the living together of two dissimilar organisms, especially when mutually beneficial"—but the example of the bird that picks food from the crocodile's teeth, thereby feeding itself and keeping the crocodile cavity-free, helps bring it home.

Classifications and Listings

A third tool frequently utilized in texts is classifications and listings. Classifying is the process by which common subjects are categorized under a general heading.

Here are two examples:

There are four seasons: winter, spring, summer, and fall.
Classification: seasons
Listing: winter, spring, summer, fall

There are four time zones in the United States: Eastern, Central, Mountain, and Pacific.
Classification: U.S. time zones
Listing: Eastern, Central, Mountain, Pacific

Especially in technical writing, authors use classification to categorize extensive lists of detail. Such writings may have several categories and subcategories that organize these details into some manageable fashion.

Comparing/Contrasting

A fourth tool used in communicating difficult information is that of comparing and contrasting. Texts use this tool to bring complicated material into focus by offering a similar or opposing picture.

Such devices are invaluable in grasping concepts that do not conjure a picture in your mind. Gravity, for example, is not something that can be readily pictured—it's not a tangible object that can be described.

Through comparison, a text relates a concept to one that has been previously defined—or to one a reader may readily understand. Through contrast, the text concentrates on the differences and distinctions between two ideas. By focusing on distinguishing features, these ideas become clearer as one idea is held up against another.

Cause-Effect Relationships

A final tool that texts employ to communicate is the cause-effect relationship. This device is best defined in the context of science, where it is the fundamental quest of most scientific research.

Science begins with the observation of the effect—what is happening? For instance, say it is snowing.

The next step is to conduct research into the cause: Why is it snowing? Detailing this cause-effect relationship is often the essence of scientific and technical writing.

Cause-effect relationships may be written in many ways. The effect may be stated first, followed by the cause. An effect may be the result of several connected causes—a causal chain. And a cause may have numerous effects.

In your reading, it is vital that you recognize this relationship and its significance.

Read with a Plan

More than any other type of writing, highly specialized technical writing must be read with a plan. You can't approach your reading assignment merely with the goal of completing it. Such mindless reading will leave you confused and frustrated, drowning in an ocean of theory, concepts, terms, and examples.

Your plan should incorporate the following guidelines:

1. Learn the terms that are essential to understanding the concepts presented. Knowing the precise definitions that the author uses will enable you to follow his chain of thought through the text.

2. Determine the structure or organization of the text. Most chapters have a definite pattern that forms the skeleton of the material. A book may begin with a statement of a theory, give examples, provide sample problems, then summarize. Often this pattern can be discerned through a preview of the table of contents or the titles and subtitles.

3. Skim the chapter to get a sense of the author's viewpoint. Ask questions to define your purpose in reading. Use any summaries or review questions to guide your reading.

4. Complete a thorough analytical reading of the text. Do not proceed from one section to the next until you have a clear understanding of the section you are reading—the concepts generally build upon each other. To proceed to a new section without understanding the ones that precede it is, at best, futile.

5. Immediately upon concluding your thorough reading, review! Write a summary of the concepts and theories you need to remember. Answer any questions raised when you skimmed the text. Do the problems. If possible, apply the formulas.

Technical material is saturated with ideas. When reading it, you must be convinced of one fact: Every individual word counts! You will want to read such material with the utmost concentration—it is not meant to be sped through.

Good readers know that such material demands a slow read that concentrates on achieving the greatest level of retention.

- Every definition has to be digested.
- Every formula must be committed to memory.
- Every example needs to be considered.

To improve your reading of such technical material, you will want to hone the skill of identifying the devices an author uses to communicate. In so doing, you will be able to connect the chain of thought that occurs. When reading such texts—or attempting to work out technical problems—try the following "tricks":

- Whenever you can, "translate" numbers and formulae into words. To test your understanding, try to put your translation into different words.
- Even if you're not particularly visual, pictures can often help. You should try translating a particularly vexing math problem into a drawing or diagram.

- Before you even get down to solving a problem, is there any way for you to estimate the answer or, at least, to estimate the range within which the answer should fall (greater than 1, but less than 10)? This is the easy way to at least make sure you wind up in the right ballpark.

- Play around. There are often different paths to the same solution, or even equally valid solutions. If you find one, try to find others. This is a great way to increase your understanding of all the principles involved.

- When you are checking your calculations, try working backwards. I've found it an easier way to catch simple mathematical errors.

- Try to figure out what is being asked, what principles are involved, what information is important, and what is not.

- Teach someone else. Trying to explain mathematical concepts to someone else will quickly pinpoint what you really know or don't know. It's virtually impossible to get someone else—especially someone who is slower than you at all this stuff—to understand if you don't!

CHAPTER 6

BECOMING A CRITICAL READER

You will find that there are many times, particularly in comparative literature classes, when you will need to read something with great care in order to remember details and interpret meaning. Hester Prynne's red monogram, Poe's talking raven, and Samuel Beckett's mysterious friend all require a little more analysis than a superficial interpretation of props and plot.

Yet such detailed, analytical reading is not limited to literature. Political dissertations, historical analyses, and even scientific research may require more careful reading than the latest "space opera."

Such reading is often referred to as critical reading, a type of reading during which you seek to distinguish thoughts, ideas, or concepts—each demanding thorough study and evaluation.

Critical reading requires that you are able to identify the author's arguments, measure their worth and truth, and apply what is pertinent to your own experience. Unlike skimming, critical reading challenges the reader to concentrate at the highest level possible. Critical readers become critical thinkers.

And critical thinkers:

1. Are honest with themselves.

2. Resist manipulation.

3. Overcome confusion.

4. Ask questions.

5. Base their judgements on evidence.

6. Look for connections between subjects.

7. Are intellectually independent.

Prepare Yourself to Read Critically

When preparing to read critically, you must lay the groundwork for concentration. Just as an athlete must ready himself mentally to achieve peak performance, you will want to ready yourself before you begin to read.

To prepare to read critically:

1. You must have a clearly defined purpose for reading. Identify it before you begin.

2. Pay attention! Minimize distractions and interruptions.

3. Find your optimum study environment—a quiet corner in the library, your own room, wherever. In absolute silence, or with your new CD playing.

4. Do not concern yourself with how fast or slowly you read. Your goal should be to understand the material, not to see how fast you can get it over with.

5. If it seems that you will need several hours to complete your reading, break it into smaller, more manageable parts, then reward yourself at the end of each of these sections with a brief break.

If you take these steps prior to reading any text that requires your utmost concentration, you will find that your mind is readied for the kind of focus necessary to read critically. Make a habit of such preparations and you will set yourself up to succeed.

Prereading Is a Must

Once you have prepared your mind to read, the next step is to understand the big picture—what is the author's thesis or main idea? Good comprehension is the consequence of your ability to grasp the main point of what the author is trying to communicate.

And grasping this message is accomplished through skimming the text, as we discussed in Chapter 4. Let's review the basic steps:

1. If there is a title or heading, rephrase it as a question. This will support your purpose for reading.

2. Examine all subheadings, illustrations, and graphics, as these will help you identify the significant matter within the text.

3. Read the introductory paragraphs, summary, and any questions at the end of the chapter.

4. Read the first sentence of every paragraph. In Chapter 3 you learned that this is generally where the main idea is found.

5. Evaluate what you have gained from this process: Can you answer the questions at the chapter's end? Could you intelligently participate in a class discussion of the material?

6. Write a brief summary of what you have learned from your skimming.

Now, Read It

Once you identify and understand the basic skeleton of the material, your actual "read" of the material—following the details, reasoning, and chain of thought—is simply a matter of attaching meat to the bones.

This digestive process involves learning to interpret and evaluate what is written, what is directly stated, and what can be inferred from the context.

Effective analytical reading requires that you, the reader, distinguish the explicit, literal meaning of words (denotation) and what suggestions or intentions are hinted at by the general content (connotation).

Analyzing: What the Words Connote

Words and writing have two levels of meaning that are important to the reader's comprehension.

The first level is the literal or descriptive meaning. What a word expressly denotes means the specific, precise definition you'd find in the dictionary.

Connotation involves this second level of meaning—that which incorporates the total significance of the words.

What does that mean? Beyond a literal definition, words communicate emotion, bias, attitude, and perspective. Analyzing any text involves learning to interpret what is implied, just as much as what is expressly stated.

15 Questions to Help You

Beyond grasping the meaning of words and phrases, critical reading requires that you ask questions. Here are 15 questions that will help you effectively analyze and interpret most of what you read:

1. Is a clear message communicated throughout?
2. Are the relationships between the points direct and clear?
3. Is there a relationship between your experience and the author's?
4. Are the details factual?
5. Are the examples and evidence relevant?
6. Is there consistency of thought?
7. What is the author's bias or slant?
8. What is the author's motive?
9. What does the author want you to believe?
10. Does this jibe with your beliefs or experiences?
11. Is the author rational or subjective?
12. Is there a confusion between feelings and facts?
13. Are the main points logically ordered?
14. Are the arguments and conclusions consistent?
15. Are the explanations clear?

Obviously, this list of questions is not all-inclusive, but it will give you a jump start when critical reading is required. Remember, the essential ingredient in any effective analysis and interpretation is the questions you ask.

Summarizing: The Final Step

Nothing will be more important to your recall than learning to condense what you read into a clear and concise summary.

Many of you have learned to do this by excerpting entire segments or sentences from a text—certainly not a very efficient method for summarizing. I recommend using the traditional outline.

Another suggestion is to use a two-step process called diagramming, which calls for the reader to diagram or illustrate the content he's just read, then write a brief synopsis of what he's learned.

Similar to outlining, diagramming helps the reader to visualize the relationships between various thoughts and ideas. Concept diagrams, or concept trees, are very useful visual aids for depicting the structure of a textbook.

Unless you have a photographic memory, you will find that recalling a picture of the main points will greatly increase what you remember. Beyond this, such diagrams require that you distill what is essential to the text and how it relates to the main message.

Suppose you read a chapter in your language arts class about the types of sciences. Your diagram might reduce your reading material to look like the following:

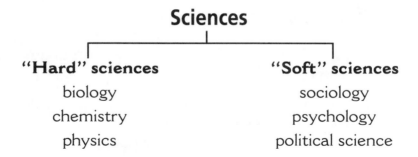

More than just a listing of main points, a diagram allows you to picture how parts fit together, which enhances your ability to recall the information you've read. This is especially true the more "visual" you are.

Distill It Into a Synopsis

The second step in the process of summarizing is to write a brief synopsis of what you've learned. When you need to review the material, diagrams will remind you of the significant elements in the text. Your synopsis will remind you of the main idea.

The goal here is to put in your own words what you gleaned from what you have read. You will find this process an invaluable gauge of whether you have understood the message—and on what level.

Use this method one chapter at a time, and do not proceed to the next chapter until you have completed the following exercise:

1. Write definitions of any key terms you feel are essential to understanding the topic.

2. Write questions and answers you feel clarify the topic.

3. Write any questions for which you don't have answers—then make sure you find them through rereading, further research, or asking another student or your teacher.

4. Even if you still have unanswered questions, move on to the next section and complete numbers 1 to 3 for that section. (And so on, until your reading assignment is complete.) See if this method doesn't help you get a better handle on any assignment right from the start.

Critical reading is not easy. It requires a lot more concentration and effort than the quick reference reading that you can get away with for much of your day-to-day class assignments. And I won't kid you—much of the reading you'll do in the latter years of high school and throughout college will be critical reading.

But if you follow the steps I've outlined for each critical reading assignment that you tackle—preparing yourself for the read, doing a preread skim followed by an analytical reading, concluding with a summarization—you'll discover that critical reading can be a much smoother, even rewarding, experience!

The Method You Probably Learned

If you were taught a specific reading method in school, it was probably the one developed back in the 1940s that is abbreviated "SQ3R." This stands for Survey, Question, Read, Recite, and Review. Here's how the process works.

Survey. Preread the chapter, concentrating on topic sentences, subheads, and review questions in order to get an overview of what's ahead.

Question. Once you've surveyed the chapter, ask yourself what information is contained in it. Consider turning the subheads into questions as an exercise.

Read. Now read the first section thoroughly, attempting to answer the questions you've posed. Take notes, highlight, underline, map.

Recite. Now answer the questions without looking at your notes or the text. When you're done, go on to the next section. Continue this detailed reading/ reciting tandem until you finish the chapter (or the assignment).

Review. Go back over the entire assignment.

Does this sound familiar? I agree. I think this method is completely incorporated into the steps I've outlined in this and previous chapters. Frankly, I think the detailed method I've proposed—and the helpful advice along the way—covers far more ground.

CHAPTER 7

READING THE LITERATURE

"Will you walk a little faster?" said a whiting to a snail. "There's a porpoise close behind us and he's treading on my tail!"

"If I'd been the whiting," said Alice, whose thoughts were still running on the song, "I'd have said to the porpoise, 'Keep back, please; we don't want you with us!'"

"They were obliged to have him with them," the Mock Turtle said. "No wise fish would go anywhere without a porpoise."

"Wouldn't it really?" said Alice in a tone of great surprise.

"Of course not," said the Mock Turtle. "Why, if a fish came to me, and told me he was going on a journey, I should say, 'With what porpoise?'"

"Don't you mean 'purpose'?" said Alice.

"I mean what I say," the Mock Turtle replied in an offended tone.

—Lewis Carroll, *Alice in Wonderland*

In this excerpt, you could enjoy the nonsensical picture of a porpoise pushing a snail and whiting to walk faster. You might laugh at the confusion of "porpoise" and "purpose" by the Mock Turtle. Or you could discern the message—that you need to have a purpose when you are on a journey… or reading.

Why should you care about literature? Who needs to read the book when you can see the movie?

While I didn't write this book to give you a lecture on the merits of the classics, please bear with me for a couple of paragraphs.

The Greatest Involvement Device

Unlike anything else, literature involves the reader in the story. How? There are no joysticks to manipulate, no "surround sound" to engulf you. Your imagination is your only involvement device, but it far surpasses any high-tech computer gimmick.

Your imagination makes reading the ultimate adventure. It allows you to immerse yourself in the story—identifying with the protagonist, fighting his battles, experiencing his fears, sharing his victories. You may become so involved, you end up staying up well past your bedtime, turning page after page late into the night!

Your imagination is the vehicle that allows you to explore a million different lives, from floating down the Mississippi River on a raft, to suffering through a star-crossed love affair, to having tea with the March Hare and Mad Hatter, as our Alice did.

Creative writing may be serious or humorous or sublime... or all three. It is often subtle; meanings are elusive and delicate. Such writing, when done effectively, evokes emotional responses. You get angry. You shed a tear. You chuckle. An author's expression strikes a chord that moves you. You and the author communicate on a level that is far beyond an exchange of facts and information.

Assuming that I have converted all you literature skeptics to avid library loiterers (and even if I haven't), I'll offer some advice to help you begin your journey to literary appreciation. It begins with understanding the basic road map.

Which Reading Method? Pleasure or Critical?

While I certainly encourage you to approach your reading with the enthusiasm and anticipation that would justify the pleasure-reading method (see Chapter 2), the demands of the teacher who assigns the reading will probably require the critical reading method.

Reading literature requires most of the skills we've discussed previously. There are devices and clues to ferret out that will help you follow the story and understand its meaning better. You will analyze and interpret what the author is saying and evaluate its worth.

But in addition, in literature you will be able to appreciate the words themselves. In textbooks, you often must penetrate a thick jungle of tangled sentences and murky paragraphs to find the information you seek.

Great literature is its language. It's the flow and ebb of its words, the cadence of its sentences, as much as it is story and theme.

As you read more, you'll uncover the diversity of tapestries that different authors weave with words. You may discover similar themes coursing through the works of authors like Ernest Hemingway or Thomas Hardy, but their use of language is as different as desert and forest. The composition of the words themselves is an element you'll want to examine as you read literature critically.

Fiction: Just Another Word for Storytelling

Most fiction is an attempt to tell a story. There is a beginning, in which the characters and the setting are introduced. There is a conflict or struggle (middle) that advances the story to a climax (end), where the conflict is resolved. A final denouement or "winding up" clarifies the conclusion of the story.

Your literature class will address all of these parts using literary terms that are often more confusing than helpful. The following are brief definitions of some of the more important ones.

Plot: The order or sequence of the story—how it proceeds from the opening through the climax. Your ability to understand and appreciate literature depends upon how well you follow the plot—the story.

Characterization: The personalities or characters central to the story—the heroes, heroines, and villains. You will want to identify the main characters of the story and their relationships to the struggle or conflict.

Theme: The controlling message or subject of the story; the moral or idea that the author is using the plot and characters to communicate. Some examples: man's inhumanity to man; man's impotency in his environment; the corrupting influence of power, greed, and unrequited love. Just as with nonfiction, you need to discern this theme to really understand what it is the author wants to communicate.

Setting: The time and place in which the story takes place. This is especially important when reading a historical novel or one that takes you to another culture.

Point of view: Who is telling the story? Is it one of the central characters giving you flashbacks or a first-person perspective? Or is it a third-person narrator offering commentary and observations on the characters, the setting, and the plot? This person moves the story along and gives it an overall tone.

The first step in reading literature is to familiarize yourself with these concepts, and then try to recognize them in each novel or short story you read.

The second step is the same as for reading nonfiction—to identify your purpose for reading.

Allow your purpose to define how you will read. If you are reading to be entertained, then a pleasure read is the way to go. If you're reading for a class and will be required to participate in discussions or be tested on the material, you'll want to do a critical read.

How Long Should It Take?

As a general rule, fiction is not meant to be read over a period of months—or even weeks. Try to read an assigned book or story as quickly as possible, fast enough to progress through the plot, get a sense of the characters and their struggles, and hear the author's message or theme.

It's helpful to set a goal as to when you want to finish your reading. Frequently, of course, this will already be set for you, if your reading is a class assignment.

You should, however, set daily goals. Set aside one or two hours to read, or set a goal of reading three chapters a day until you finish. Reading sporadically—10 minutes one day, a half hour the next, then not picking up the book until several days later—means that you'll lose track of the plot and characters and just as quickly lose interest.

Too often, when students do not establish a regular schedule, their reading becomes fragmented, making it very difficult to piece together the whole story. A reasonable goal is to try to read a novel in less than a week, a short story in one sitting.

If you try to read fiction more rapidly, you will greatly increase your enjoyment of it. It is vitally important that as you try to read faster, you give the story your full attention. By doing this you will be surprised by how improved your understanding and appreciation are.

To speed your reading of fiction, try this experiment:

1. Find a novel or short story that interests you and is relatively easy to read. Tomes like *Ulysses* or *The Naked Lunch* shouldn't be candidates.

2. Set aside two or three hours to invest in reading the book. If at all possible, finish it in one sitting. If you can't, then allocate the same amount of time each day until you do.

By trying this experiment, you will discover that fiction is intended to be read this way—in one sitting, whenever possible. It is as if you are sitting at a master storyteller's feet as he spins his tale. You want to know how the story ends and what happens to the hero.

Will the villain get his comeuppance? Will the hero get the girl? Or will he ride off with his horse?

You'll find that you appreciate the story far more at the end than anywhere in the middle.

Some other tips for reading fiction:

1. Understand the plot and maintain awareness of its progression.

2. Take breaks to review what has occurred and who is involved.

3. Vary your reading method, from skimming transitional bridge material to carefully reading descriptions and narration.

4. Question the story's theme. What is the message?

You're Allowed to Enjoy It

A final recommendation: Give yourself permission to enjoy what you are reading. You will be amazed at the difference this will make. Fiction, unlike any other reading, can take you on an adventure. Through your mind, you can journey to faraway lands, pretend you are someone else, feel emotions you may never otherwise experience. All this happens as you gain an appreciation of literature—as you learn to understand fiction and allow yourself to enjoy great stories.

CHAPTER 8

FOCUSING YOUR MIND

Unlike other activities, reading requires an active mind and a passive body. A deadly combination, especially when you've spent the day in classes and haven't had a chance to burn off that excess energy with a tennis match, a game of "hoops," or a quick run around campus.

Concentration-wise, reading can be more demanding than class lectures, homework assignments, or taking notes. In class, you at least have vocal variety and the threat of being called on to keep you focused. And writing, while a sedentary activity, still requires some hand-eye coordination to keep your brain working.

Keep Your Mind on One Thing

Concentration begins with the ability to keep your mind focused on one thing—your reading assignment. This is not an innate talent, but a learned discipline. Much like an athlete must learn to be so focused that she is completely unaffected by screaming crowds, a good reader absorbs himself in what he's reading.

How does your mind discipline "rate"? Answer these questions to find out:

1. When I read, do I often allow random thoughts to steal my focus?

2. As I read, am I easily distracted by noises or other activities?

3. Am I watching the clock to see how long I have to keep reading?

There is no simple, magic formula for conjuring up concentration—especially when you're faced with a critical reading assignment you're not particularly enamored of. But if you follow the preparatory steps I've discussed in previous chapters—define your purpose, skim for a pre-read, identify questions for which you will seek answers—you should find it a bit easier to stay focused.

Steps to Better Concentration

Here are some other practical steps I recommend to increase your ability to concentrate:

1. **Get some exercise** before you begin your reading. A game of racquetball, an exercise class, a workout at the gym, even a brisk walk, will help burn off physical energy so you'll be able to direct all of your mental energy to your reading.

2. **Read in the right place.** No, it's not in front of the TV, nor in your room if your roommate is hosting a pizza party. Reading is a solitary activity. Find a quiet corner, preferably in a place designated for study only—at your desk or in the library. Although tempting, reading on your bed can be dangerous if you're struggling to concentrate. You just may lose the battle and find yourself in the perfect place to doze off.

3. **Eliminate distractions.** If you've properly scheduled your reading time, you won't be distracted by other pending assignments. If you're trying to read one assignment while worrying about another, your concentration—and comprehension—will inevitably suffer.

   Make sure there's nothing else in sight to vie for your attention. Are there letters on your desk that you need to answer? Put them away and schedule some time to write back. Do you hear sirens and screams from the TV show in the other room? Turn it off or down or, better yet, close your door.

4. **Plan breaks.** If you have three hours or more of reading ahead of you, the mere thought of it may be so discouraging that you'll lose your concentration before you even pick up the book. Schedule short 10- or 15-minute breaks after each hour of reading. Get up. Listen to some music. Stretch. If you must break more frequently, keep your breaks shorter. By dividing your reading into smaller, more digestible bites, you'll be able to concentrate more effectively.

Wait! Don't Start Reading Yet

Have you defined your purpose for reading? Once again, you must have a clearly defined purpose or goal. What are you reading for? (I have addressed this numerous times, but spaced repetition is a very effective way to make a point.) The point is that reading without purpose is the greatest means to getting nowhere, which is where you'll find your mind after about a half-hour.

Know why you are reading. If your teacher or professor has given you questions to answer, then you know what you're looking for. If not, ask your own questions, using the clues in your book (as discussed in Chapter 2).

An effective preread of the material should help you define your purpose and stimulate some interest in finding out more—which will result in increased concentration.

Motivation: Crucial to Concentration

Motivation is key to your success in just about any endeavor, whether it's graduating with honors, maintaining an effective time-management program, or improving your reading. You can utilize all the tricks and steps I've mentioned in this chapter, but if you lack the motivation to read, you'll still find it a struggle to concentrate on your assignments.

There are two types of motivation—intrinsic and extrinsic. What's the difference?

An avid murder mystery fan, you buy stacks of paperbacks at the used bookstore and spend your free time with your nose buried in them. You love the challenge of figuring out who's guilty before you reach the end. In fact, you'd spend all weekend reading mysteries if you didn't have to complete a reading assignment for your political science class. You're not particularly interested in that course, but your efforts on this assignment could secure you an A for the term, so you're determined to read the material and "ace" the exam.

Your motivation for reading the mysteries is intrinsic— you do it because you enjoy it. You don't get any awards. You don't get paid for it.

The poly sci reading, on the other hand, requires external motivation. You're reading it because you want to earn a high grade in class. Your reward is external—beyond the reading itself.

Whether you are intrinsically motivated to read or doing it for some external reward doesn't matter, as long as you are motivated by something! If you find it difficult to get excited about reading your economics assignment, remind yourself of how this exercise will help your grade. Get yourself externally motivated.

If that doesn't get you motivated enough to read for three hours, there's nothing wrong with a little bribery. Reward yourself with something more immediate. Promise yourself that if you stay focused on your reading until it's completed, you can rent the movie you've been wanting to see, or you can buy that new CD. (If you need lots of extrinsic motivation, you could run out of money!)

The value of concentration can be summed up in one statement: Concentration is essential to comprehension. Where there is failure to focus, there will be little or no understanding.

Without concentration, you will see only words on a page.

CHAPTER 9

RETAINING THE INFORMATION

The ultimate test of your comprehension is what you remember after you have finished your reading.

As a student, most of your reading will be for classes in which, sooner or later, you'll be required to regurgitate the information you've read in some type of format—essay test, term paper, multiple-choice, true/false, or fill-in-the-blank final.

So, beyond just being able to complete your reading assignments, you want to be sure you remember what you've read.

All of you have probably had the experience of forgetting that one fact that made the difference between an A- and a B+ (or a B- and a C+). It was sitting right there, on the tip of your brain, but you couldn't quite remember it.

Memory Can Be Improved

You probably know people with photographic (or near-photographic) memories. They know all the words to every song recorded in the last four years, remind you of things you said to them three years ago, and never forget anyone's birthday (or anniversary or "day we met" or "first kiss day," ad infinitum).

While some people seem to be able to retain information naturally, a good memory—like good concentration—can be learned. You can control what stays in your mind and what is forgotten.

Some people remember with relative ease and have no problem retaining large volumes of information. Others often are aggravated by a faulty memory that seems to lose more than it retains. Several factors contribute to your capability to recall information you take in.

- **Intelligence, age, and experience** all play a role in how well you remember. Not everyone remembers the same way. You need to identify how these factors affect your memory and learn to maximize your strengths.

- **Laying a strong foundation** is important to good memory. Most learning is an addition to something you already know. If you never grasped basic chemistry, then mastering organic chemistry will be virtually impossible. By developing a broad foundation of basic knowledge, you will enhance your ability to recall new information.

- **Motivation is key** to improving your memory. A friend of mine, the consummate baseball fan, seems to know every baseball statistic from the beginning of time. He can spout off batting averages and ERAs from any decade for virtually any player, his favorite team's season schedule…and most of the other teams', too! While I wouldn't say he is the most intelligent guy I've ever met, he obviously loves baseball and is highly motivated to learn everything he can about his favorite subject. You probably have a pet interest, too. Whether it's movies, music, or sports, you've filled your brain with a mountain of information. Now, if you can learn that much about one subject, you are obviously capable of retaining information about other subjects—even chemistry. You just have to learn how to motivate yourself.

- **A method, system, or process** for retaining information is crucial to increasing your recall. This may include organizing your thinking, good study habits, or mnemonic devices—some means that you utilize when you have to remember.

- **Using what you learn** right after you learn it is important to recall. It's fine to memorize a vocabulary list for a quick quiz, but if you wish to retain information for the long haul, you must reinforce your learning by using this knowledge. For example, you will add a new word to your permanent vocabulary if you make a point to use it, correctly, in a conversation.

The study of foreign languages, for many, proves frustrating when there are no opportunities outside of class to practice speaking the language. That's why foreign language students often join conversation groups or study abroad—to reinforce retaining what they've learned by using it.

Why We Forget

As you think about the elements of developing good memory, you can use them to address why you forget. The root of poor memory is usually found in one of these areas:

1. We fail to make the material meaningful.
2. We did not learn prerequisite material.
3. We fail to grasp what is to be remembered.
4. We do not have the desire to remember.
5. We allow apathy or boredom to dictate how we learn.
6. We have no set habit for learning.
7. We are disorganized and inefficient in our use of study time.
8. We do not use the knowledge we have gained.

All of us are inundated with information every day, bombarded with facts, concepts, and opinions. We are capable of absorbing some information simply because the media drench us with it. In order to retain most information, we have to make a concerted effort to do so. We must make this same effort with the material we read.

How to Remember

There are some basic tools that will help you remember what you read:

- **Understanding.** You will remember only what you understand. When you read something and grasp the message, you have begun the process of retention. The way to test this is to rephrase the message in your own words. Can you summarize the main idea? Unless you understand what is being said, you won't be able to decide whether to remember or discard it.

- **Desire.** Let me repeat: You remember what you choose to remember. If you do not want to retain some piece of information or don't believe you can, then you won't! To remember the material, you must want to remember it and be convinced that you will remember it.

- **Overlearn.** To ensure that you retain material, you need to go beyond simply doing the assignment. To really remember what you learn, you should learn material thoroughly, or overlearn. This involves prereading the text, doing a critical read, and having some definite means of review that reinforces what you should have learned.

- **Systematize.** It's more difficult to remember random thoughts or numbers than those organized in some pattern. For example, which phone number is easier to remember: 538–6284 or 678–1234? Once you recognize the pattern in the second number, it takes much less effort to remember than the first. You should develop the ability to discern the structure that exists and recall it when you try to remember. Have a system to help you recall how information is organized and connected.

- **Association.** It's helpful to attach or associate what you are trying to recall to something you already have in your memory. Mentally link new material to existing knowledge so that you are giving this new thought some context in your mind.

A Procedure to Improve Recall

Each time you attempt to read something that you must recall, use this six-step process:

1. **Evaluate the material and define your purpose** for reading. Identify your interest level and get a sense of how difficult the material is.

2. **Choose appropriate reading techniques** for the purpose of your reading.

3. **Identify the important facts.** Remember what you need to. Identify associations that connect the details you must recall.

4. **Take notes.** Use your own words to give a synopsis of the main ideas. Use an outline, diagram, or concept tree to show relationships and patterns. Your notes provide an important backup to your memory. Writing down key points will further reinforce your ability to remember.

5. **Review.** Quiz yourself on those things you must remember. Develop some system by which you review notes at least three times before you are required to recall. The first review should be shortly after you've read the material, the second a few days later, and the final just before you are expected to recall. This process will help you avoid cram sessions.

6. **Implement.** Find opportunities to use the knowledge you have gained. Study groups and class discussions are invaluable opportunities to implement what you've learned.

Memorizing and Mnemonics

There are some specific methods to help you recall when you must remember a lot of specific facts. The first of these is rote memorization—the process of trying to recall information word-for-word.

Memorize only when you are required to remember something for a relatively short time—when you have a history quiz on battle dates, a chemistry test on specific formulas, or a vocabulary test in French.

When memorization is required, you should do whatever is necessary to impress the exact information on your mind. Repetition is probably the most effective method. Write down the information on a 3 × 5 card and use it as a flashcard. You must quiz yourself frequently to assure that you know the information perfectly.

A second technique for recalling lots of details is mnemonics. A mnemonic device is used to help recall large bits of information which may or may not be logically connected. Such mnemonics are invaluable when you must remember facts not arranged in a clear fashion, items that are quite complicated, and numerous items that are a part of a series.

One of the simplest methods is to try to remember just the first letter of a sequence. That's how Roy G. Biv (the colors of the spectrum, in order from left to right—red, orange, yellow, green, blue, indigo, violet) came about. Or **E**very **G**ood **B**oy **D**oes **F**ine, to remember the notes on the musical staff. Or, perhaps the simplest of all, **FACE**, to remember the notes in between. (The latter two work opposite of old Roy—using words to remember letters.) Of course, not many sequences work out so nicely. If you tried to memorize the signs of the zodiac with this method, you'd wind up with **A**ries, **T**aurus, **G**emini, **C**ancer, **L**eo, **V**irgo, **L**ibra, **S**corpio, **S**agittarius, **C**apricorn, **A**quarius, **P**isces. Many of you may be able to make a name or a place or something out of ATGCLVLSSCAP, but I can't!

One solution is to make up a simple sentence that uses the first letters of the list you're trying to remember as the first letters of each word. To remember the zodiacal signs, just memorize the phrase **A T**all **G**iraffe **C**hewed **L**eaves **V**ery **L**ow; **S**ome **S**low **C**ows **A**t **P**lay.

Wait a minute! It's the same number of words. Why not just figure out some way to memorize the signs themselves? What's better about the second set? A couple of things. First of all, it's easier to picture the giraffe and cow and what they're doing. Creating mental images is a very powerful way to remember almost anything. Second, because the words in our sentence bear some relationship to each other, they're much easier to remember. Go ahead, try it. See how long it takes you to memorize the sentence as opposed to all the signs. This method is especially easy when you remember some or all of the items but don't remember their order.

Remember: Make your sentence(s) memorable to you. Any sentence or series of words that helps you remember these letters will do. Here are just two more I created in a few seconds: **A T**all **G**irl **C**alled **L**ovely **V**era **L**oved to **S**ip **S**odas from **C**ans **A**nd **P**lates. **A**ny **T**iny **G**erbil **C**ould **L**ove **V**enus. **L**ong **S**illy **S**nakes **C**ould **A**ll **P**ray. (Isn't it easy to make up memorably silly pictures in your head for these?)

You will find that in business or the classroom, mnemonic devices like this allow you to readily recall specific information that you need to retain for longer periods of time. They are especially useful if you have to remember chemical classifications, lines of music, and anatomical lists.

As effective as mnemonic devices are, don't try to create them for everything you have to remember. Why? To generate a device for everything you need to learn would demand more time than any one person has. And you just might have trouble remembering all the devices you created to help you remember in the first place! Too many mnemonics can make your retention more complicated and hinder effective recall.

Complex mnemonics are not very useful—they can be too difficult to memorize. When you choose to utilize a mnemonic, you should keep it simple so that it facilitates the quick recall you intended.

Many people complain that their mind is a sieve—everything they read slips through—and they never remember anything. I hope you now are convinced that this is a correctable problem. You don't have to be a genius to have good retention— you simply must be willing to work at gaining the skills that lead to proficient recall. As you master these skills, you will improve your reading by increasing your rate of retention.

Chapter 10

Let's Read Up on ADD

W hat is ADD (Attention Deficit Disorder)? It's probably easiest to describe as a person's difficulty with focusing on a single thing for any significant period of time. People with ADD are described as easily distracted, impatient, impulsive, and often seeking immediate gratification. They have poor listening skills and trouble doing "boring" jobs (like sitting quietly in class or, as adults, balancing a checkbook). "Disorganized" and "messy" are words that also come up often.

Hyperactivity, however, is more clearly defined as restlessness, resulting in excessive activity. Hyperactives are usually described as having "ants in their pants." ADHD is a combination of hyperactivity and ADD.

According to the American Psychiatric Association, a person has ADHD if he or she meets eight or more of the following paraphrased criteria:

1. Can't remain seated if required to do so.

2. Is easily distracted by extraneous stimuli.

3. Focusing on a single task is difficult.

4. Frequently begins another activity without completing the first.

5. Fidgets or squirms (or feels restless mentally).

6. Can't (or doesn't want to) wait for his turn during group activities.

7. Will often interrupt with an answer before a question is completed.

8. Has problems with chore or job follow-through.

9. Can't play quietly easily.

10. Impulsively jumps into physically dangerous activities without weighing the consequences.

11. Easily loses things (pencils, tools, papers) necessary to complete school or work projects.

12. Interrupts others inappropriately.

13. Talks impulsively or excessively.

14. Doesn't seem to listen when spoken to.

Three caveats to keep in mind: The behaviors must have started before age seven, not represent some other form of classifiable mental illness, and occur more frequently than in the average person of the same age.

Characteristics of People with ADD

Let's look at the characteristics generally ascribed to people with ADD in more detail:

Easily distracted. Since ADD people are constantly "scoping out" everything around them, focusing on a single item is difficult. Just try having a conversation with an ADD person while a television is on.

Short, but very intense, attention span. Though it can't be defined in terms of minutes or hours, anything ADD people find boring immediately loses their attention. Other projects may hold their rapt and extraordinarily intense attention for hours or days.

Disorganization. ADD children are often chronically disorganized—their rooms are messy, their desks are a shambles, their files incoherent. While people without ADD can be equally messy and disorganized, they can usually find what they are looking for; ADDers can't.

Distortions of time sense. ADDers have an exaggerated sense of urgency when they're working on something and an exaggerated sense of boredom when they have nothing interesting to do.

Difficulty following directions. A new theory on this aspect holds that ADDers have difficulty processing auditory or verbal information. A major aspect of this difficulty involves the very common reports of parents of ADD kids who say their kids love to watch TV and hate to read.

Daydreaming, falling into depressions, or having mood swings.

Take risks. ADDers seem to make faster decisions than non-ADDers.

Easily frustrated and impatient. ADDers do not beat around the bush or suffer fools gladly. They are direct and to the point. When things aren't working, "Do something!" is the ADD rallying cry, even if that something is a bad idea.

Why Do ADD Kids Have Trouble in School?

What should you look for in a school setting to make it more palatable to an ADDer? What can you do at home to help your child (or yourself)?

- **Learning needs to be project- and experience-based,** providing more opportunities for creativity and shorter and smaller "bites" of information. Many "gifted" programs offer exactly such opportunities. The problem for many kids with ADD is that they've spent years in nongifted classroom settings and may be labeled with underachieving behavior problems, effectively shut out of the programs virtually designed for them! Many parents report that children diagnosed as ADD, who failed miserably in public school, thrived in private school. What characterizes many private schools? Smaller classrooms and more individual attention with specific goal-setting, project-based learning. These factors are just what make ADD kids thrive!

- **Create a weekly performance template** on which both teacher and parent chart the child's performance, positive and negative.

- **Encourage special projects for extra credit.** Projects give ADDers the chance to learn in the mode that's most appropriate to them. They will also give such kids the chance to make up for the "boring" homework they sometimes simply can't make themselves do.

- **Stop labeling them as "disordered."** Kids react to labels, especially negative ones, even more than adults do.

■ **Think twice about medication,** but don't discard it as an option. Many experts are concerned about the long-term side effects of the drugs normally prescribed for ADDers. On the other hand, if an ADD child cannot have his special needs met in a classroom, not medicating him may be a disaster.

Specific Suggestions About Reading

■ **Practice, practice, practice.** ADDers will tend to have trouble reading, preferring visual stimulation to the "boring" words. Turn off the TV. Minimize time spent with PlayStation or other such games. ADDers may well be extraordinarily focused on such visual input and stimulating games, but only to the detriment of their schoolwork. Where possible, though, utilize videos, computers, interactive multimedia, and other forms of communication more attuned to ADDers to help them learn. There is a tremendous amount of educational software and CD-ROM material that may work better for ADDers than traditional printed books.

However, ADDers must obviously learn to read and practice reading. I would suggest finding a professional or a program to deal with your or your child's probable reading problems. Anything you can do to make reading more fun and interesting should be explored.

■ **Break everything into specific goal units.** ADDers are very goal-oriented; as soon as they reach one, it's on to the next. Reestablishing very short-term, "bite-size" goals is essential. Make goals specific, definable, and measurable, and stick to only one priority at a time.

- **Create distraction-free zones.** Henry David Thoreau (who evidently suffered from ADD, by the way) was so desperate to escape distraction he moved to isolated Walden Pond. Organize your time and workspace to create your own "Walden Pond," especially when you have to read, write, take notes, or study. ADDers need silence, so consider the library. Another tip: Clean your work area thoroughly at the end of each day. This will minimize distractions as you try to read.

- **Train their attention span.** ADDers will probably never be able to train themselves to ignore distractions totally, but a variety of meditation techniques might help them stay focused longer.

- **Utilize short-term rewards.** ADD salespeople don't do well when a sales contest lasts for 6 months, even if the reward is, say, a 10-day cruise. But stick a $100 bill on the wall and watch them focus! Those with ADD are not motivated by rewards that are too ephemeral or too far in the future. They live for the here and now and need to be rewarded immediately.

I want to thank Thom Hartmann, author of *Attention Deficit Disorder: A Different Perception* (Underwood Books, 1997), from which I have freely and liberally borrowed (with his permission) for this chapter.

CHAPTER 11

BUILD YOUR OWN LIBRARY

"The reading of all good books is like
conversation with the finest men of past centuries."
—Descartes

I f you are ever to become an active, avid reader, access to books will do much to cultivate the habit. I suggest you "build" your own library. Your selections can and should reflect your own tastes and interests, but try to make them wide and varied. Include some of the classics, contemporary fiction, poetry, and biographies.

Save your high school and college texts—especially those from any English composition or writing classes. You'll be amazed at how some of the material retains its relevance. And try to read a good newspaper every day so as to keep current and informed.

Your local librarian can refer you to any number of lists of the "great books," most of which are available in inexpensive paperback editions. Here are four more lists—compiled by yours truly—of "great" classical authors; "great" not-so-classical authors, poets, and playwrights; some contemporary "pretty greats"; and a selection of my own favorite "great" books.

You may want to incorporate these on your to-buy list, especially if you're planning a summer reading program.

I'm sure that I have left off someone's favorite author or "important" title from these lists. So be it. They are not meant to be comprehensive, just relatively representative. I doubt anyone would disagree that a person familiar with the majority of authors and works listed would be considered well-read!

Who are Derek Walcott, Kenzaburo Oe, Nadine Gordimer, Octavio Paz, and Camilo Jose Cela? All winners of the Nobel Prize for Literature (1989 to 1994, along with Toni Morrison in 1993). I'm willing to bet a year's royalties not one of you reading this has heard of more than one of them (with the exception of Ms. Morrison). So how do you define "great" if these award winners are so anonymous? I include this merely to dissuade another 200 or so letters castigating me for some of those authors or works I did include in these lists.

Some "Great" Classical Authors

Aeschylus	Chaucer	Hegel	Pindar
Aesop	Cicero	Homer	Plato
Aquinas	Confucius	Horace	Plutarch
Aristophanes	Dante	S. Johnson	Rousseau
Aristotle	Descartes	Kant	Santayana
Balzac	Dewey	Machiavelli	Shakespeare
Boccaccio	Emerson	Milton	Spinoza
Burke	Erasmus	Montaigne	Swift
J. Caesar	Flaubert	Nietzsche	Vergil
Cervantes	Goethe	Ovid	Voltaire

Some Other "Great" Authors

Sherwood Anderson

W.H. Auden

Jane Austen

Samuel Beckett

Brandan Behan

William Blake

Bertolt Brecht

Charlotte Bronte

Emily Bronte

Pearl Buck

Samuel Butler

Lord Byron

Albert Camus

Lewis Carroll

Joseph Conrad

e.e. cummings

Daniel Defoe

Charles Dickens

Emily Dickinson

John Dos Passos

Feodor Dostoevski

Arthur Conan Doyle

Theodore Dreiser

Alexandre Dumas

Lawrence Durrell

George Eliot

T.S. Eliot

William Faulkner

Edna Ferber

F. Scott Fitzgerald

Ford Madox Ford

E.M. Forster

Robert Frost

John Galsworthy

Jose Ortega y Gasset

Nikolai Gogol

Maxim Gorki

Thomas Hardy

Nathaniel Hawthorne

Ernest Hemingway

Hermann Hesse

Victor Hugo

Aldous Huxley

Washington Irving

Henry James

William James

James Joyce

Franz Kafka

M.M. Kaye

John Keats

Rudyard Kipling

Arthur Koestler

D.H. Lawrence

Jack London

H.W. Longfellow

James Russell Lowell

Thomas Mann

W. Somerset Maugham

Herman Melville

H.L. Mencken

Henry Miller

H.H. Munro (Saki)

Vladimir Nabokov

O. Henry

Eugene O'Neill

George Orwell

Dorothy Parker

Edgar Allan Poe

Ezra Pound

Marcel Proust

Ellery Queen

Ayn Rand

Erich Maria Remarque

Bertrand Russell

J.D. Salinger

George Sand

Carl Sandburg

William Saroyan

Jean Paul Sartre

George Bernard Shaw

Percy Bysshe Shelley

Upton Sinclair

Aleksandr I. Solzhenitsyn

Gertrude Stein

Robert Louis Stevenson

Dylan Thomas

James Thurber

J.R.R. Tolkien

Leo Tolstoy

Ivan Turgenev

Mark Twain

Robert Penn Warren

Evelyn Waugh

H.G. Wells

Walt Whitman

Oscar Wilde

Thornton Wilder

Tennessee Williams

P.G. Wodehouse

Thomas Wolfe

Virginia Woolf

William Wordsworth

William Butler Yeats

Emile Zola

Some "Pretty Great" Contemporary Authors

Edward Albee

Isaac Asimov

James Baldwin

John Barth

Saul Bellow

T. Coraghessan Boyle

Anthony Burgess

Truman Capote

John Cheever

Don DeLillo

Pete Dexter

E.L. Doctorow

J.P. Donleavy

William Gaddis

William Golding

Dashiell Hammett

Robert Heinlein

Joseph Heller

Lillian Hellman

John Hersey

Oscar Hijuelos

Jerzy Kozinski

Malcolm Lowry

Norman Mailer

Bernard Malamud

Gabriel Garcia Marquez

Cormac McCarthy

Carson McCullers

Toni Morrison

Joyce Carol Oates

Flannery O'Connor

Thomas Pynchon

Philip Roth

Isaac Bashevis Singer

Jane Smiley

Wallace Stegner

Rex Stout

William Styron

Anne Tyler

John Updike

Alice Walker

Eudora Welty

Some "Great" Works

The Adventures of
    Huckleberry Finn

The Aeneid

Aesop's Fables

The Age of Innocence

The Alexandra Quartet

Alice in Wonderland

All the King's Men

All Quiet on the Western
    Front

An American Tragedy

Animal Farm

Anna Karenina

Arrowsmith

As I Lay Dying

Atlas Shrugged

Babbitt

The Bell Jar

Beloved

Beowulf

The Bonfire of the Vanities

Brave New World

The Brothers Karamazov

The Canterbury Tales

Catch-22

The Catcher in the Rye

A Clockwork Orange

Confessions of an English
    Opium Eater

The Confessions of Nat Turner

The Count of Monte Cristo

Crime and Punishment

David Copperfield

Death Comes for the
    Archbishop

Death of a Salesman

The Deerslayer

Demian

Don Juan

Don Quixote

Ethan Fromme

Far from the Madding Crowd

A Farewell to Arms

The Federalist Papers

The Fixer

For Whom the Bell Tolls

The Foundation

From Here to Eternity

The Ginger Man

The Good Earth

The Grapes of Wrath

Gravity's Rainbow

The Great Gatsby
Gulliver's Travels
Hamlet
Heart of Darkness
Henderson the Rain King
The Hound of the Baskervilles
I, Claudius
The Idiot
The Iliad
The Immortalist
The Invisible Man
Jane Eyre
JR
Julius Caesar
Kim
King Lear
Lady Chatterley's Lover
"Leaves of Grass"
The Legend of Sleepy Hollow
Les Miserables
A Long Day's Journey into Night
Look Homeward, Angel
Lord Jim
Lord of the Flies
The Lord of the Rings

Macbeth
The Magic Mountain
Main Street
Man and Superman
The Merchant of Venice
The Metamorphosis
Moby Dick
The Naked and the Dead
Native Son
1984
Of Human Bondage
Of Mice and Men
The Old Man and the Sea
Oliver Twist
One Flew over the Cuckoo's Nest
The Optimist's Daughter
Othello
Our Town
Paradise Lost
The Pickwick Papers
The Picture of Dorian Gray
A Portrait of the Artist as a Young Man
Portrait of a Lady
Pride and Prejudice
The Prophet
Ragtime

"The Raven"

The Red Badge of Courage

The Remembrance of
      Things Past

The Return of the Native

Robinson Crusoe

Romeo and Juliet

The Scarlet Letter

Siddhartha

Silas Marner

Sister Carrie

Slaughterhouse Five

Sons and Lovers

Sophie's Choice

The Sound and the Fury

Steppenwolf

A Streetcar Named Desire

The Sun Also Rises

The Tale of Genji

A Tale of Two Cities

Tender Is the Night

The Thin Red Line

The Time Machine

A Thousand Acres

Tom Jones

The Trial

Ulysses

U.S.A. (trilogy)

Vanity Fair

Walden

War and Peace

"The Wasteland"

The Way of All Flesh

Wuthering Heights

Reading every one of these books will undoubtedly make you a better reader; it will certainly make you more well-read. The added bonus to establishing such a reading program is an appreciation of certain authors, books, cultural events, and the like that separates the cultured from the merely educated and the undereducated.

Read on and enjoy.

CHAPTER 12

READING:
A LIFELONG ACTIVITY

"And further, by these, my son, be admonished:
making many books there is no end..."
—Solomon (Ecclesiastes 12:12)

W ell, you made it through another book. I hope you found the motivation—whether intrinsic or extrinsic—to define your purpose, discern the important details, grasp the main idea, and retain what you read. I promised not to preach about the joys of reading. And I haven't...too much.

Your need to read—and comprehend and retain what you read—will not end when you graduate from school.

Planning on working? From the very first week, when you're given the employee handbook, you'll be expected to seek out the facts—like what happens if you're late more than twice.

You'll be required to read critically—and understand the meaning of statements like "Our dress code requires professional attire at all times."

Business proposals, annual reports, patient charts, corporate profiles, product reports, sales reports, budget proposals, business plans, resumes, complaint letters, interoffice memos—no matter what type of work you do, you won't be able to avoid the avalanche of paper and required reading that accompanies it.

Not only will your job require the ability to read and comprehend, but so will other facets of your life. If you plan to buy a house, wait until you see the pile of paperwork you'll have to wade through.

Credit card applications? Better read the fine print to make sure you know when your payment must be in...and how much interest you're paying on that brand-new TV.

Insurance policies, appliance warranties, local ordinances, newspapers, membership applications, and tax forms—it seems like any goal you pursue in your life will require you to scale mountains of reading material.

For your own best interest, you must be prepared to read—and understand.

I wish you the greatest possible success in your future reading pursuits, of which there will be many...throughout your life.

Glossary

analgesic Relating to the relief of pain.

assimilate To take in information and understand it fully.

cultivate To develop a skill.

cumbersome Difficult to use or carry due to large size.

denigrate To criticize strongly or unfairly; belittle.

discern To perceive or recognize.

doggedly Persistently.

extolling Praising highly.

futile Useless or ineffective.

glean To gather information gradually.

inconsequential Insignificant or trivial.

insidious Spreading harmful effects gradually.

inundated Overwhelmed with.

osmosis Gradual assimilation of ideas; also the process through which molecules pass through a membrane.

paramount Most important or superior.

ponderous Having great weight; labored and awkward.

quagmire A complicated situation that is difficult to get out of.

scintillating Witty, clever, or brilliant.

sedentary Inactive; tending to stay in a seated position.

surmount To overcome an obstacle.

vested Guaranteed, as rights or benefits assigned to a person.

FOR MORE INFORMATION

Center for the Book
Library of Congress
101 Independence Avenue S.E.
Washington, DC 20540-4920
(202) 707-5221
Web site: http://www.read.gov
The Center for the Book in the Library of Congress invites people
of all ages to discover the fascinating people, places and events
that await you whenever you read.

The College Board
250 Vesey Street
New York, NY 10281
(212) 713-8000
Website: https://www.collegeboard.org
The College Board is a mission-driven not-for-profit organization
that connects students to college success and opportunity. Each
year, the College Board helps more than seven million students
prepare for a successful transition to college through programs
and services in college readiness and college success—including the
SAT and the Advanced Placement Program. The organization also
serves the education community through research and advocacy
on behalf of students, educators, and schools.

International Literacy Institute (ILI)
University of Pennsylvania
Graduate School of Education
3700 Walnut Street
Philadelphia, PA
19104-6216
(215) 898-2100

Website: http://www.literacy.org/home
The International Literacy Institute (ILI), established by UNESCO
and the University of Pennsylvania in 1994, provides leadership in
research, development, and training in the broad field of international literacy and educational development, with an emphasis on
developing countries. Literacy.org is an important resource for
research and development on literacy in the U.S. and worldwide.

National Center for Education Statistics
Institute of Education Sciences
1990 K Street, NW
8th & 9th Floors
Washington, DC 20006
(202) 502-7300
Website: https://nces.ed.gov
The National Center for Education Statistics (NCES) is the primary
federal entity for collecting and analyzing data related to education in the U.S. and other nations. NCES is located within the U.S.
Department of Education and the Institute of Education Sciences.
NCES fulfills a Congressional mandate to collect, collate, analyze,
and report complete statistics on the condition of American education; conduct and publish reports; and review and report on education activities internationally.

U.S. Department of Education
400 Maryland Avenue, SW
Washington, DC 20202
1-800-USA-LEARN (1-800-872-5327)
Website: http://www.ed.gov
The U.S. Department of Education's mission is to promote student
achievement and preparation for global competitiveness by foster-
ing educational excellence and ensuring equal access.

Websites

Because of the changing nature of Internet links, Rosen Publishing
has developed an online list of websites related to the subject of
this book. This site is updated regularly. Please use this link to
access this list:

http://www.rosenlinks.com/SSS/Read

FOR FURTHER READING

Athans, Sandra K., and Robin W. Parente. *Tips & Tricks for Analyzing Text and Citing Evidence* (The Common Core Readiness Guide to Reading). New York, NY: Rosen Publishing, 2015.

Athans, Sandra K., and Robin W. Parente. *Tips & Tricks for Evaluating an Argument and Its Claims* (The Common Core Readiness Guide to Reading). New York, NY: Rosen Publishing, 2015.

Armstrong, Linda. *Common Core Language Arts Workouts, Grade 8*. Quincy, IL: Mark Twain Media, 2015.

Bromberg, Murray, and Melvin Gordon. *1100 Words You Need to Know.* 6th ed. Hauppage, NY: Barron's Educational Series, 2013.

Cameron, Schyrlet, and Suzanne Myers. *Assessment Prep for Common Core Reading: Tips and Practice for the Reading Standards.* Quincy, IL: Mark Twain Media, 2015.

Cornog, Mary W. *Merriam-Webster's Vocabulary Builder.* Merriam-Webster's, 2010.

Greenberg, Michael. *Painless Vocabulary* (Painless Series). 2nd ed. Hauppage, NY: Barron's Educational Series, 2011.

Guare, Richard, Peg Dawson, and Colin Guare. *Smart But Scattered Teens: The "Executive Skills" Program for Helping Teens Reach Their Potential.* New York, NY: The Guilford Press, 2013.

Jones, Darolyn. *Painless Reading Comprehension* (Painless Series). 2nd ed. Hauppage, NY: Barron's Educational Series, 2012.

Killcoyne, Hope, ed. *Great Authors of Popular Fiction* (Essential Authors for Children & Teens). New York, NY: Britannica Educational Publishing, 2014.

Lugo, Monica P. *McGraw Hill's 500 SAT Critical Reading Questions to Know by Test Day.* New York, NY: McGraw Hill Education, 2014.

Maats, Hunter, and Katie O'Brien. *The Straight-A Conspiracy: Your Secret Guide to Ending the Stress of School and Ruling the World.* Los Angeles, CA: 368 Press, 2013.

Muchnik, Claudia Clumeck, and Justin Ross Muchnik. *Straight-A Study Skills.* Avon, MA: Adams Media, 2013.

Nagle, Jeanne, ed. *Great Authors of Classic Literature* (Essential Authors for Children & Teens). New York, NY: Britannica Educational Publishing, 2014.

Nagle, Jeanne, ed. *Great Authors of Nonfiction* (Essential Authors for Children & Teens). New York, NY: Britannica Educational Publishing, 2014.

Princeton Review. *Word Smart.* 5th ed. Framingham, MA: Princeton Review, 2012.

INDEX

G

gathering facts, 47–61
Get Rich Slow, 24
goals
for ADD readers, 109
time spent reading literature,
86–87
good readers, definition of, 3–5
graphs, 20
guidelines, reading, 68–70

H

habits, creating, 3, 10
Hardy, Thomas, 84
Hartmann, Thom, 110
heads, chapters, 18–19
Hemingway, Ernest, 84
highlighted terms, 20, 39
Hollywood Urban Legends, 56
Homework Helpers: Biology, 49
How to Study Program, 39
hyperactivity, 105. *See also* **ADD**
(Attention Deficit Disorder)

I

ideas
building blocks (facts), 48
finding, 33–45
gathering facts, 48
identifying topic sentences, 34–37
imagination, 82–83
impatience, 107
implementing knowledge learned,
101
improving
comprehension, 5–9
concentration, 89–91

memory, 96–97
reading skills, 109–110
recall skills, 100–101
skills, motivation to, 2–3
vocabularies, 9
increasing. *See also* **improving**
comprehension, 10–11
retention rates, 12
speed, reading, 9–10
indexes, 18
information, retaining, 95–103.
See also **reading**
intelligence, 96
interpreting critical reading,
75–76
introductions, 17
involvement devices, 82–83

K

key words, 9
King, Stephen, 13, 23

L

lead-ins, 18
learning
sequential, 10
skills, 96
levels of meaning, 74
libraries, building, 111–118
listings, 64, 66
literature
critical or pleasure-reading
methods, 83–84
enjoying, 88
involvement devices, 82–83
reading, 82–88
time spent reading, 86–87

About the Author

Ron Fry is a nationally known spokesperson for the improvement of public education and an advocate for parents and students playing an active role in strengthening personal education programs. In addition to being the author of the vastly popular *How to Study Program*, Fry has edited or written more than 30 different titles—resources for optimum student success.